ADVANCE PRAISE
FOR *HIGH POINT*

The poster child for town making! HIGH POINT is North America's most teachable new community. To now have Tom Phillips' inspirational book *High Point* to provide the back story, philosophy and achievement is a remarkable treat. Each year I bring thirty people from all parts of America to the Pacific Northwest to see the best of the best in walkable, livable, sustainable, equitable, affordable town making, and High Point sets the bar high. Having walked or worked on more than twenty of the best walkable villages in America, I find High Point the most remarkable of all. Tom's new book completes the picture.

—Dan Burden, Director of Innovation and Inspiration, Blue Zones

I have had the privilege of representing High Point through nearly a quarter century in public service. Tom Phillips' excellent history brings together the many milestones we have celebrated together in this unique community. This is a story of an urban neighborhood designed and built with a commitment to inclusion, environmental stewardship, and engagement. High Point remains true to its aspirational name—a place that represents the best of what we can accomplish together.

—Dow Constantine, King County Executive

Where we live has a profound effect on our health and well-being. The High Point Community in Seattle has led the way in showing us how to create places that are good for people and the planet. Tom Phillips developed a pioneering vision for a neighborhood that provides people from diverse racial, cultural, and class backgrounds with the opportunity to live in healthy and green homes, connected to each other, in a setting that protects the local environment. He led a nine-year initiative to transform a deteriorating and dangerous public housing site into a vibrant, mixed-income, green, walkable, and healthy community connected to the surrounding neighborhood. He describes his journey from concept to completion with engaging candor and detail, bringing to life the successes, mistakes, and challenges along the way. Balancing the interests of the public housing residents living on the site, owners of market-rate homes, government and housing authority officials, designers, and construction companies was no mean feat. His attention to centering development on community-building and equity and respecting the wisdom of public housing residents in the design process is noteworthy. It is marvelous to see the weaving together of New Urbanist design principles, innovative natural surface water drainage and other environmental approaches, and healthy and green building design practices into an integrated, holistic community master plan. Tom drew on all his skills and experiences, from the Peace Corps to community organizing to urban planning to project management, to pull it off. This is the story of how he did it.

—Dr. James Krieger, MPH, is founding Executive Director of Action for Healthy Food (AHF) and Institute for Healthy Food (IHF) and was chief of the Chronic Disease and Injury Prevention Section at Public Health-Seattle and King County

High Point demonstrated that it was possible to rethink how we deliver access to affordable housing that benefits people and the planet. An early visit to High Point gave me the confidence to continue pushing within Enterprise Community Partners to ensure that the Green Communities Criteria would be comprehensive. This book takes the reader inside the groundbreaking development process used as Tom and the Seattle Housing Authority set an important precedent in our collective journey to listen to communities and co-design dignified and environmentally beneficial neighborhoods that work for the people who call them home.

—Dana Bourland, Vice President, Environment, The JPB Foundation, Former Vice President of Green Initiatives Enterprise Community Partners

Tom Phillips has done a tremendous service to the field of mixed-income development by capturing his cherished experience of nine years as the lead project manager for the High Point redevelopment in Seattle in such exquisite detail. This is a highly informative and enjoyable read for anyone interested in a caring, honest insider's account of the task of transforming an isolated public housing development into a thriving, environmentally-friendly mixed-income community.

—Mark L. Joseph, PhD, Associate Professor. Leona Bevis and Marguerite Haynam Professorship in Community Development Founding Director, National Initiative on Mixed-Income Communities. Jack, Joseph and Morton Mandel School of Applied Social Sciences. Case Western Reserve University

High Point is an important story that needs to be told. A neighborhood that had been a landing place for generations of newcomers to Seattle was physically worn-out and needed a careful set of hands to steer it to become a sustainable, integrated, and successful new community. Enter Tom Phillips and the team from Seattle's Housing Authority. With creative energy and strong resolve they accomplished just that, and for the first time connected it to the larger community which surrounds it. A wonderful legacy!

—Greg Nickels, 51st Mayor of Seattle

Tom Phillips has given us a gift that can be unwrapped to reveal many hidden surprises. His book is an engaging and heroic tale about the challenges of New Urbanist community-building. This is an important history and truth-telling, about a community that stands today as a replicable model for affordable sustainability.

—Lucia Athens, City of Austin Chief Sustainability Officer

High Point tells the story of a transformational community redevelopment from the inside—an intimate look at the issues, elements, people and leadership that it takes to wrangle the many complex elements of declining public housing into a national inspiration. It's an important contribution to the redevelopment literature.

—Jonathan F. P. Rose, Author, *The Well-Tempered City*,
urban planner and developer

You had said you wanted to write an accessible book so people could understand some lessons, and that is what you did. The complexity of building a green, healthy, mixed-income housing development has never been explained so simply. This is a manual for turning design and community aspirations into reality, reflecting the negotiations, expertise, and cooperation between multiple agencies, an integrated design team, and contractors. Phillips does not minimize the financial risk that public housing authorities embrace when developing housing using private market methods, a riskiness that can limit innovation and the production of a successful neighborhood. Nonetheless, he traces the achievement of goals from lofty ideas to practical implementation. He talks the reader not only through how to use green construction practices to create an environmentally sustainable neighborhood but also how to include community feedback, thoughtful tenant relocation, and a commitment to the consideration of the social impacts of financial decisions to create a community that includes a mix of incomes and ethnicities.

—Rachel Garshick Kleit, PhD, Professor of City
and Regional Planning, Ohio State University

As the Executive Director for Neighborhood House, one of the key social service organizations at High Point, I had a front-row seat to the entire redevelopment process. I got to know and work closely with Tom Phillips on the design and construction of the High Point Neighborhood Center and came to appreciate his attention to detail and commitment to a bold vision, but most of all his genuine love for this unique community. This book chronicles the success of High Point through Tom's tenacious leadership.

—Mark Okazaki, Neighborhood House
Executive Director (2000–2019)

High Point tells the story of how a neighborhood was transformed from being considered dangerous and a place to avoid into a safe, walkable, sustainable, beautiful and diverse neighborhood to live, work, and play in. This extraordinary story is a step-by-step case study on development done right. It portrays an intimate view of the successes and failures of a multiyear process. It showcases the cooperation and input of the existing residents combined with outside experts, partnerships with architects and engineers, the utility department, environmentalists and health professionals, who, under Tom Phillips' planning and design leadership, transformed High Point into a neighborhood where families are now buying homes, moving into apartment buildings, using the library, and enjoying the trees, green spaces, and an energy-efficient community building.

The redevelopment of High Point faced every problem that confronts city councils, planning and community development departments, and housing authorities in neighborhoods that are lower income, deteriorating and perceived as dangerous. This is a book that should be read by every municipal official, planner, urban designer, developer and home owner. Once started, it is hard to put down. It is well written and illustrated, extraordinarily informative and results-driven, proving that the problems confronting older cities can be solved with the right process. It is a process that needs to be emulated.

—Tony Nelessen, M Arch UD, PP, CNU, Professor of Urban Planning and Design, Emeritus Program Director of Urban Planning and Design, Planning and Public Policy and Public Health, Bloustein School of Planning and Public Policy, Rutgers University

HIGH POINT

The Inside Story of Seattle's First
Green, Mixed-Income Neighborhood

TOM J. PHILLIPS

Splash Block Publishing

Copyright © 2020 Tom J. Phillips

ALL RIGHTS RESERVED

No part of this book may be translated, used, or reproduced in any form or by any means, in whole or in part, electronic or mechanical, including photocopying, recording, taping, or by any information storage or retrieval system without express written permission from the author or the publisher, except for the use in brief quotations within critical articles and reviews.

www.highpointbook.com

Limits of Liability and Disclaimer of Warranty:
The authors and/or publisher shall not be liable for your misuse of this material. The contents are strictly for informational and educational purposes only.

Warning—Disclaimer:
The purpose of this book is to educate and entertain. The authors and/or publisher do not guarantee that anyone following these techniques, suggestions, tips, ideas, or strategies will become successful. The author and/or publisher shall have neither liability nor responsibility to anyone with respect to any loss or damage caused, or alleged to be caused, directly or indirectly by the information contained in this book. Further, readers should be aware that Internet websites listed in this work may have changed or disappeared between when this work was written and when it is read.

Published by Splash Block Publishing
Printed and bound in the United States of America

ISBN: 978-0-578-62622-2
Library of Congress Control Number: 2020905599

DEDICATION

To Milo for your steadfast support and wise guidance
throughout the eighteen-year High Point adventure

FOREWORD
BY RON SIMS

We can mistakenly ignore the power of a community. They live and breathe. The streets, houses, sidewalks, trees, flowers, and open spaces affect our sense of personal and family well-being. A neighborhood can be a pleasant or a harrowing memory. High Point was accepted as a neighborhood with very little promise. Moving out of the neighborhood became the hope of many. The physical and mental health of a community is directly affected by the look and feel of a neighborhood. Major financial institutions saw the area as a risky investment. High Point had to overcome skepticism and decades of indifference from both residents, visitors, and local and regional government. In their chambers and offices they would quietly describe it as a place of monumental challenges that were unlikely to be overcome. It was easy to ignore that the physical and mental health of a community are directly affected by the look and feel of a neighborhood.

Tom Phillips was not going to accept the status quo. He knew there was a greatness in the community. It was the perfect place to rethink and redo design and investment. It would also require Neighborhood House to significantly add to its missions. He had to dream on behalf of the residents of the community without losing their support. This book is a masterful lesson for all who read it. Silence can be overcome by organizing and enabling a community's voice and hopes. The High Point of today was once just a dream. It is now a thriving and vibrant community. The residents walk taller and the children are proud to say that they live in High Point. It is a community that buried its stigma under parks, playgrounds, new schools, trees, lighting, viewpoints and walkable streets. High Point is a lesson for the design of any neighborhood. It has become a place where children and family flourish. Some will say, How far has High Point moved from its past? Neighborhood House became the vehicle for the hopes and dreams of the voiceless. It empowered a community and altered its direction. Many of us say, It has moved at light speed from its past. Yet, the rich ethnic diversity and cultures of the neighborhood remain. This book will inspire others to act upon their dreams.

—Ron Sims, Former Deputy Secretary of United States Department of Housing and Urban Development, also former King County Executive

TABLE OF CONTENTS

TABLES

INTRODUCTION

H*igh Point: The Inside Story of Seattle's First Green, Mixed-Income Neighborhood* is a detailed account of how a master-planned, mixed-income redevelopment in West Seattle became a poster child for green affordable housing. This story examines the circumstances that contributed to making High Point a breakout community that would later provide a basis for determining other green communities. The professionals who created the LEED for Neighborhood Development[1] checklist used High Point as their prototype.

As project manager of the High Point redevelopment, I spent nine years on the front lines setting the tone and guiding the evolution of our approach to the redevelopment. In this book I share how the process of planning and building the community affected me as well as how I influenced what High Point has become. I propose that designing and constructing quality green affordable housing requires considering factors over and beyond resource conservation. Quality design is enhanced by community input and green decisions. Using fewer resources and the right products is of paramount importance, but a health-promoting environment, quality design, and community engagement should have equal weight in the planning and building process.

---

[1] LEED stands for Leadership in Energy and Environmental Design. U.S. Green Building Council, "LEED certification for neighborhood development," accessed August 26, 2019, https://new.usgbc.org/leed/rating-systems/neighborhood-development.

The fourteen chapters in the book cover the wide array of topics that are part of creating and operating a new community. Although this book follows the general timeline of main redevelopment events, the chapters are arranged thematically rather than chronologically. Themes covered include the Seattle Housing Authority and HOPE VI grants; moving low-income families during redevelopment; greening and reconstruction; the multifaceted organizations required to manage a site of this size; and marketing middle-income homes built next to low-income homes. The book concludes with a series of interviews with current High Point residents to give readers a firsthand impression of what living at High Point is like today.

It is my hope that this book will inspire the next generation of urban planners and sustainability advocates to be creative and think big in terms of what can be accomplished in community building and green development. *High Point* is a record not only of the lessons my team and I learned during the redevelopment but also of the value of perseverance and taking many small steps while holding firmly to a vision. The story of High Point is the story of a diverse community, sustainability, and teamwork coalescing and coming to life. It is a story of how the land itself shapes the spaces we call home.

I would like to acknowledge that High Point is on the traditional land of the first people of Seattle, the Duwamish People past and present, and honor with gratitude the land itself and the Duwamish Tribe.

PART 1
THE BEGINNING

High Point: Timeline of Key Events

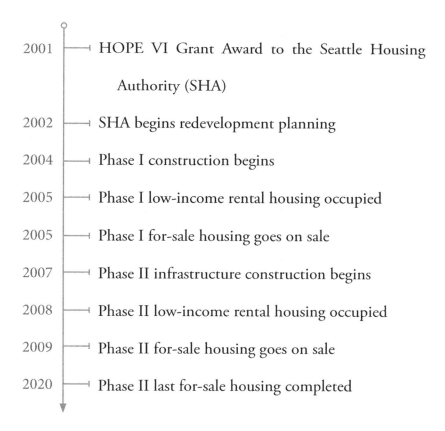

2001 — HOPE VI Grant Award to the Seattle Housing Authority (SHA)

2002 — SHA begins redevelopment planning

2004 — Phase I construction begins

2005 — Phase I low-income rental housing occupied

2005 — Phase I for-sale housing goes on sale

2007 — Phase II infrastructure construction begins

2008 — Phase II low-income rental housing occupied

2009 — Phase II for-sale housing goes on sale

2020 — Phase II last for-sale housing completed

Some of the Awards Given to High Point

- Energy Star: 2006 Outstanding Achievement Award

- 2007 Rudy Bruner Award for Urban Excellence: Silver Medalist

- Puget Sound Regional Council: 2007 Vision Award

- PCBC 2007 Gold Nugget Award:
  Master-planned community of the year

- 2007 Governor's Smart Communities—Jury Merit Award

- EPA 2007 National Award for Smart Growth Achievement

- Urban Land Institute: 2007 Award of Excellence—Americas

- Urban Land Institute: 2007 Award of Excellence—World

CHAPTER 1

HIGH POINT

The newly built community for WW II plane and ship workers in the 1940s.

Meet High Point

High Point comes to its name legitimately. At 520 feet (160 meters) above sea level, it is the highest point in Seattle.[2] Height

[2] The highest point proper is actually across the street from the redevelopment site, at a City of Seattle reservoir tower.

in Seattle translates into magnificent views of snowcapped mountains and sparkling bodies of water. Great views are usually taken advantage of in order to increase the value of real estate. Although high real estate values and affordable housing may seem like unusual bedfellows, they make for a long-term successful relationship in the High Point story: how a fifty-year-old once-wartime housing project became home to a diverse population of working-class families, immigrants, and refugees; eventually fell into disrepair; and was revitalized as a master-planned, mixed-income neighborhood that became a poster child for green affordable housing.

At 120 acres (over 480,000 square meters), High Point is a large, highly-prized piece of real estate. Walking time across the site—twenty-five minutes from north to south, and eight minutes from east to west—provides a way to understand its scale. High Point has always had the most important ingredient for a successful real estate development: location. It sits in the middle of West Seattle, a neighborhood located on a peninsula to the west and south of central Seattle. About 11 percent of Seattle's 710,000-strong population live in greater West Seattle. In addition to High Point's sweeping views of the east of Puget Sound and downtown Seattle, the site offers good access to the downtown and south King County business hubs. It is about a ten-minute drive from the center of High Point to downtown Seattle during non-peak traffic hours. The community enjoys pleasant parks and saltwater beaches and has a reputation for being a great place to raise a family.

High Point Diaries

The video documentary *The Diaries of High Point,* created in 2002 by Gary Thomsen and his Chief Sealth High School class, provides a window into the lives of High Point residents from 1942 to the turn of the century. *Diaries* depicts four different eras.

Footage from the first era, the 1940s through the early 1950s, shows both the uncertainties of residents during World War II and their dedication to the war effort. From the cemetery neighboring High Point, soldiers flew dirigibles to ward off bombing attacks. During this phase, High Point provided inexpensive housing for working families, with some enjoying indoor plumbing and kitchens for the first time. The Seattle Housing Authority (SHA) assumed ownership of High Point from the federal government in the early 1950s, and the site remained a low-income housing neighborhood.

During the second phase, which ran up to the late 1960s, High Point was, by many accounts, a well-functioning, cohesive, mixed-income community. Some families describe this period nostalgically as a time when everyone looked after everyone else. It was the kind of place where children could play throughout High Point rather than having to stay on their own block. Where there was a contest for best garden every summer, and the family that took first place won a month's free rent. Elizabeth Stubblefield, who grew up at High Point, was sentimental about that older community: "I truly loved growing up in High Point." She then raised a family in the community from 1962 to 1976.

According to Elizabeth's son Marcus, who was interviewed for *Diaries*, "[When we did something we should not have], our parents would hear about it an hour before we got home."

In 1969, the US Congress passed the Brooke Amendment, which placed an income limit on families moving into public housing and capped the rent level that housing authorities could charge at 25 percent (later 30 percent) of a family's income. This heralded a third and difficult phase at High Point. The Brooke Amendment resulted not only in the concentration of low-income families in certain areas but also discouraged families from earning more income so as to avoid higher rent payments.

One of the unanticipated consequences of the amendment and other changes governing public housing was that housing authorities were unable to increase rents and therefore did not have adequate resources to maintain the housing or sites. The federal government made some attempts to make up for this shortcoming in the form of rent supplements and modernization funding, but these efforts were also underfunded and insufficient to adequately maintain large sites such as High Point. In the following years, the US Department of Housing and Urban Development added criteria that further affected who was eligible to live in public housing.[3]

During a severe recession in Seattle in the late 1970s, SHA was unable to fill the units with renters and reduced the original 1,300 units at High Point to around 750 units.[4] SHA accomplished this

---

[3] Ron Atkielski, personal interview with author, July 21, 2015.
[4] Seattle Housing Authority, 2002.

by clearing several blocks on the southwest end of the site and tearing down units within existing blocks. This reduced the site to its present 120 acres and also changed the site's configuration.

The 1990s, the fourth and last period described in *Diaries*, was a low point for the High Point community. This period saw the influx of both crack cocaine and gangs in Seattle, which made the High Point neighborhood dangerous, especially after sundown. Former resident Allan Stowers summarized these conditions in the documentary: "I've seen stabbings and [gun] shots. Individuals were not to be trusted." However, even during this period, a sense of community existed among longtime High Point residents. The majority of residents went about their daily lives and coped with the violence around them.

The Seattle Housing Authority

The Seattle Housing Authority, which owns High Point, is not a City of Seattle department. It is a separate government agency, established in 1939 as part of the New Deal federal legislation.[5] Like the approximately 3,400 other housing authorities in the country, SHA is authorized and primarily funded by the federal Department of Housing and Urban Development (HUD).[6]

---

[5] Cassandra Tate, "Seattle Housing Authority Chronology," HistoryLink,org, April 10, 2014, https://www.historylink.org/File/10774.
[6] US Department of Housing and Urban Development, "Public Housing: Image versus Facts," accessed August 26, 2019, https://www.huduser.gov/periodicals/ushmc/spring95/spring95.html.

SHA is one of thirty-nine housing authorities nationally participating in the HUD Moving to Work program. Moving to Work (MTW) "allows the [public housing] agency to test innovative methods to improve housing services and to better meet local needs."[7] The MTW program gives certain housing authorities "wide discretion in the design of program fundamentals (for example, rent formulas and time limits on receipt of housing assistance) as well as in the use of funds."[8] And because the redevelopment used funds from multiple sources (for example, State of Washington, proceeds from land sales, etc.; see Table 1), the housing authority was not subject to HUD's traditional cost limits on such categories as unit costs.[9]

SHA's approach to financing the High Point redevelopment centered around "[leveraging] the HOPE VI grant with tax-exempt bond issues that generate 4 percent tax credit equity."[10]

TABLE 1. Financing the High Point redevelopment

Funding source	Amount
Private investment	$285,000,000
Other public funding	$106,000,000
Tax-exempt funding	$68,000,000
Tax credit partnership equity	$56,000,000
HOPE VI grant	$35,000,000
Total	**$550,000,000**

---

[7] Seattle Housing Authority, "Moving to Work (MTW)," accessed August 26, 2019, https://www.seattlehousing.org/about-us/reports/moving-to-work-reports.
[8] Henry G. Cisneros and Lora Engdahl, eds., *From Despair to Hope, Hope VI and the New Promise of Public Housing in America's Cities* (Brookings Institution Press: Washington, DC, 2009), 268.
[9] George Nemeth, personal communication to author, April 1, 2019.
[10] Cisneros and Engdahl, eds., *From Despair to Hope*, 111.

SHA only operates in Seattle and has limited formal links to the City of Seattle government (City). In Seattle, the City has sway over the housing authority only indirectly. SHA is governed by a seven-member board of directors who are nominated by the mayor and approved by the city council. This gives the mayor and city council some influence over the housing authority, but this is much different from a regular city department where the mayor has a direct say in its operations, and the city council approves the budget and establishes policy direction. However, the city council does have a direct vote on every land-use proposal made by all city developers, including the housing authority.

SHA is primarily a residential management organization. It owns more than 8,000 apartments and single-family homes at nearly 400 sites in Seattle.[11] For the purposes of a redevelopment project, SHA has to do everything a private developer has to do to obtain the permits to build in the city. This includes participating in the same public hearing process, paying all of the same fees, and abiding by the same land-use rules. If the housing authority is lucky, it may receive the benefit of the doubt on an occasional issue, but this is not guaranteed; in fact, the housing authority can be subject to even greater scrutiny.

---

[11] Seattle Housing Authority, "SHA Housing," https://www.seattlehousing.org/housing/sha-housing.

The HOPE VI Grant Made Redevelopment Possible

By the late 1990s, SHA knew it had to do something about the problematic physical and social conditions at High Point, one of its major housing projects. High Point was not only "one of 18 drug 'hot spots'" in Seattle, it was also "housing built in 1942 that was never intended to last nearly 50 years."[12]

The HOPE VI Program was launched in 1992 by the then new Clinton administration and its HUD Secretary, Henry G. Cisneros,[13] in response to the National Commission on Severely Distressed Public Housing. The commission called for the federal government "to act immediately to eliminate conditions that cause the families—men, women, and children—living in approximately 86,000 units of severely distressed public housing to reside in physical, emotional, social, and economic distress."[14]

There are mixed views on the HOPE VI Program. HOPE VI transformed, on a large scale, highly unsafe and unhealthy housing that was occupied primarily by people living in poverty. HOPE VI has operated in 240 neighborhoods across the country and provided 111,059 new and remodeled

---

[12] High Point HOPE VI Application, May 18, 2000, 17.
[13] Cisneros and Engdahl, eds., *From Despair to Hope.*
[14] "The Final Report of the National Commission on Severely Distressed Public Housing: A Report to the Congress and the Secretary of Housing and Urban Development," Washington, DC, August 1992.

housing units, 59,674 (53.7 percent) of which were affordable for low-income public housing families. On the other hand, critics have accused HOPE VI partners of trying to "break up minority communities."[15]

In 2001, HUD announced a $35 million HOPE VI grant to SHA. This was one of the financial pieces that made the High Point redevelopment possible. However, this money alone was insufficient for SHA to proceed. Something else was needed. That something else was a commitment from HUD to provide SHA with monthly financial assistance that would allow the 600 low-income families who would live in the redeveloped High Point to pay only 30% of their monthly income for rent and utilities.

HUD's commitment to pay the balance—the difference between what the tenants could afford and the actual costs to the housing authority—was essential to making the project financing work. It made lenders comfortable, knowing that the income from renters plus the rent subsidy would be sufficient to maintain the rental properties. HUD established ceilings for these monthly rental subsidies that SHA could not exceed. This meant that SHA had to bring the rental costs (debt payments and operational costs) within the parameters established by HUD. The HUD grant money would also help to pay SHA costs of building the infrastructure on the site: roads, sewers, power lines, streetlights, etc.

---

[15] Cisneros and Engdahl, eds., *From Despair to Hope,* 290.

Another source of income, which the total project budget depended on, was money from the sale of land to private for-sale housing builders, as part of creating a mixed-income development. This meant that we had to balance the pressures to be prudent and keep our costs down with the need to create a total site that was appealing and featured enough amenities to make it attractive to homebuyers.

While this funding model seems secure and relatively risk-free, it depends on all of the pieces falling into place on time in a cash flow sequence. The income must be available soon after the expenses are incurred. This would turn out to be the exact problem we would face during the Great Recession (see Chapter 11).

HOPE VI Grants in Seattle

Prior to receiving the grant for High Point, SHA had secured HOPE VI grants for its two other former WWII military worker housing communities, Holly Park (renamed NewHolly) and Rainier Vista. In order to redevelop these sites, SHA needed to take on a new role: developer of a master-planned community. A master-planned community is a large residential plan that includes numerous recreational and commercial amenities.

In this new capacity, SHA had to change the zoning within High Point and secure other approvals, called entitlements,

This page showing deteriorated conditions was part of the successful HOPE VI application to HUD.

from the City of Seattle. The process of obtaining entitlements turned out to be a training ground for all the players involved: city council, SHA, neighbors living on or near the site, other affordable housing providers in Seattle, the mayor's office, and city departments. These organizations all had a stake in the outcome of the review process, which was where they could influence important elements of the redevelopment.

Some of the more important issues raised at NewHolly and settled for all three sites included:

- SHA would provide one-for-one replacement housing for every unit that existed at the site at the beginning of the redevelopment. That is, in Seattle, there would be a permanent replacement unit for a low-income family for every unit torn down at a HOPE VI site.
- SHA would need to demonstrate that the old units did not have unique historic value and obtain approval from the Seattle Historic Preservation Office before SHA could start construction.
- What funding sources SHA could tap into and which sources would be left for Seattle's nonprofit housing organization.[16]

Public hearings conducted by the city council would be the venue where everyone with an interest in the redevelopment plans would have a chance to speak.

---

[16] SHA agreed to not seek Seattle Housing Levy funds.

A Deep Reservoir of Experience and a Talented Consulting Team

By the time I was hired in June 2001, many of the staff at SHA had already been working on other HOPE VI projects for six years. They would prove to be an invaluable resource throughout my nine years at the housing authority. Many of the systems for hiring staff, selecting contractors, meeting minority contracting requirements, and working through convoluted HUD rules had already been put in place by experienced personnel.

At one of the many groundbreaking celebrations at High Point, I thanked each SHA staff member present for their help. It did not take long to find out that I had inadvertently left someone off my list. But I will take my chances again of providing a short list of those who played a key role in the High Point redevelopment effort and are mentioned throughout this book and offering them my gratitude.

Within SHA:

- Harry Thomas and Tom Tierney, executive directors
- Al Levine, development director
- Stephanie Van Dyke, coworker and eventually development director
- Stephen Antupit, planner for new home sales
- George Nemeth, housing planner and reservoir of all knowledge about the functioning of the housing authority

- Genevieve Aguilar and Kari-lynn Frank, two of the High Point community builders
- Julie Schaefer, ace administrative assistant
- Willard Brown, housing management guru who oversaw the management of all of the HOPE VI sites

High Point neighbors:

- Bonita Blake, High Point community leader
- Goldie Holms, High Point community leader

Outside consultants:

- Peg Staeheli, principal of SvR Design, responsible for civil engineering and some of the landscaping on the site; others at SvR include Kathy Gwilym and Dave Rodgers
- Bill Kreager and Brian Sullivan, architects with Mithun Associates, the principal site and building designer; others in Mithun who were critical to our success include Brian Cloward, Margaret Harrison, and Gabriela Frank
- Al Doyle, head of Fusion Marketing
- Tom Byers, a consultant with Cedar River Associates and friend of Dr. Jim Krieger, a Seattle-based, nationally prominent community health leader

SHA's founder and first executive director was the now deceased visionary Jesse Epstein, who built three WWII military worker housing communities: High Point, Rainier Vista, and Holly Park. He also developed Yesler Terrace. Jesse was my friend and mentor when I was growing up in Seattle.

PART 2
TAKING ON
HIGH POINT

CHAPTER 2

A DAUNTING
RESPONSIBILITY

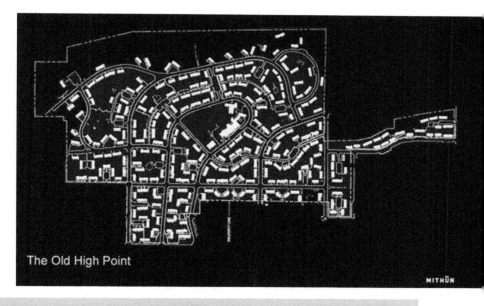

The Old High Point

MITHUN

This schematic shows the street pattern and the barracks-style housing from the original community.

Al Levine offered me the job of running the High Point redevelopment on a Friday in late August 2001. I told him I needed the weekend to think about it. I had already been working for SHA for several months, but taking on the senior project manager position responsible for the High Point redevelopment was a big step up. I would be running the city's largest redevelopment project ever. As I admitted to Al on the following Monday, I was hesitant to take the job because I was afraid I might bankrupt the housing authority. While this concern turned out to be prescient, voicing it at the time was more my way of saying indirectly, "There are big parts of this job about which I know very little. Are you sure you really want me?"

As HUD had given SHA the authority to act as its own developer at High Point, taking the senior project manager role would mean that, with support from others in the agency, I would be responsible for directing the architectural and engineering team; determining the "program" (what would be built on the site in addition to the 600 affordable housing units and a comparable number of for-sale homes); securing City entitlements (the zoning, street vacations, etc.); establishing the schedule; selecting and supervising the construction contractors; selecting the for-sale builders; and overseeing the overall marketing. Others in the development department would be responsible for securing financing, overseeing the relocation of the residents, and managing the new housing and large site. Nonetheless, my responsibilities would be daunting.

Despite my reservations, I decided that this was my dream job. It offered everything I was looking for at that point in my career, and it was an opportunity to be in charge of a large master-planned community in my hometown. I would no longer be a consultant advising developers about New Urbanism[17] for their budding communities, but the person making the major design decisions.

In addition, the job had a strong social equity element, which was important to me, and it had potential to be a significant project nationally. So I accepted the position of senior project manager and began overseeing the redevelopment of a community I hoped would be special. In fact, my wife, Julie Wade, and I had discussed buying a home in the new community. When I mentioned this to a longtime housing authority employee, she was incredulous at the thought of our moving to High Point; she could not see beyond her history of working in such a dangerous community. This was an example of some of the resistance I faced from within SHA toward the transformation we were planning for High Point. Over time, I developed my own base of support in the community, which provided me with the political cover to implement most of my ideas for High Point.

All SHA department managers report to an executive director. Not surprisingly, the largest department in the agency is operations. Maintenance personnel and residential managers work in the operations department. The development department is

---

[17] Since the early 1990s, I had been mildly obsessed with New Urbanism. I stayed up to date with the literature and had visited many of the most successful New Urbanist communities nationally; for example, Seaside, Florida; Kentlands, Maryland; Harbor Island, Tennessee, as well as Poundbury, England. "New Urbanism is a planning and development approach based on the principles of how cities and towns had been built for the last several centuries: walkable blocks and streets, housing and shopping in close proximity, and accessible public spaces. In other words: New Urbanism focuses on human-scaled urban design." ("What Is New Urbanism?" Congress for the New Urbanism, accessed July 1, 2019, https://www.cnu.org/resources/what-new-urbanism.)

much smaller. Its mission is to build any new housing, such as High Point, and then turn the completed site over to operations. In my new role, I was two levels below the executive director of the agency. My boss was the development director, and he reported directly to the executive director. In the private sector, I would have been called a developer, as I was the one making the major decisions about the redevelopment, with the exception of financing. I met weekly with the development director to review these decisions, but for the most part, my ideas carried the day.

The Right Skills at the Right Time

As it happened, I was the right person in the right job at the right time. My varied thirty-year career as an urban planner had provided me with the unique combination of knowledge and skills needed to manage Seattle's largest residential redevelopment.

To others, and sometimes even to me, it might have seemed that I had a somewhat checkered career. I did stints with the Peace Corps in Liberia and was a Vista volunteer in Lima, Ohio, where I worked with low-income families as a community organizer. I spent two years at the New School in New York City studying urban policy analysis. I also did a stretch in a politically appointed position as a manager of King County's community development office, where I learned about community development, affordable housing, and how to supervise a staff of thirty-five people.

Two of my other career stops provided me with knowledge that I frequently called upon to plan High Point. The first was with Energy Rated Homes, a nonprofit I worked with in the late '80s and early '90s that worked with mortgage lenders to incorporate a home-energy rating into the mortgage-lending process. The other involved a consulting business I ran just before I started working for SHA. In the early '90s, I was the Northwest manager for A. Nelessen Associates—a consulting practice owned by Tony Nelessen, an urban planning professor at Rutgers University—and through this role, I received an advanced course in New Urbanism. Tony created the Visual Preference Survey, a tool we used with cities in the Northwest to show that citizens favored New Urbanist ideas. Most people, when given the choice, preferred to live in a more human-scale environment—a New Urbanist environment—as opposed to one overtaken by automobiles. Over the years, that consulting business morphed into another I ran with a different planning colleague. We used visual surveys and other techniques for gauging public preferences to advise master-planned-community developers nationally on how to better plan new communities. I put this knowledge to good use at High Point.

Mr. Fox, Meet Ms. Holmes

In the spring of 2001, before I started working for SHA but after the community had learned that a redevelopment was being planned, a short but heated spat took place at a meeting of the High Point Resident Council.[18]

John Fox, head of the Seattle Displacement Coalition, had asked to be on the agenda, in the hopes of swaying the residents against the redevelopment. He told the residents that the redevelopment planned for High Point was a bad idea because of the dislocation it would cause them. He supported leaving the community as it then was, saying that, if anything were to be done, the units should be remodeled.

Goldie Holmes, a longtime High Point resident, was the president of the council at the time. Ms. Holmes, a savvy grandmother, said she thought the redevelopment was needed and a good idea.

"You have been brainwashed by the housing authority," Mr. Fox responded when Ms. Holmes defended the High Point redevelopment plans. "I have not been brainwashed," Ms. Holmes said. "I'm an army veteran, and I know what brainwashing is." At the next regular council meeting, the council approved a motion spearheaded by Ms. Holmes to prevent the Displacement Coalition from ever returning to High Point. In effect, they voted the coalition off the island.

The consequences of this vote were significant and far-reaching. The Displacement Coalition had been a thorn in the side of the housing authority's redevelopment efforts since the mid-

---

[18] I heard about this meeting from HOPE VI property manager Willard Brown. High Point resident Bonita Blake later confirmed the details.

1990s when the coalition had successfully delayed the start of the NewHolly redevelopment on a procedural issue. The coalition had also rallied a number of Rainier Valley activists and Rainier Vista residents in opposition to that community's redevelopment effort, extracting costly concessions from the housing authority.

As a result of Ms. Holmes's successful motion against the Displacement Coalition, our team was able to focus on enriching the High Point redevelopment with innovations we never could have imagined when we started. During the nine years I managed the redevelopment, I made public presentations frequently to the city council, and only once, during the final rezoning hearing, did John Fox testify. I doubt whether we would have been able to maintain our energy and enthusiasm if the Displacement Coalition had questioned SHA efforts at every turn, as had happened at NewHolly and Rainier Vista. Instead of having to defend ourselves, we were given an open field and the opportunity to enhance the redevelopment at High Point.

CHAPTER 3

CHALLENGES AHEAD

To keep the redevelopment in the news, we held frequent press events. Here dignitaries participate in an unusual groundbreaking ceremony that had them creating amended soil (used in the swales across the site) by mixing compost and a gravel mix. (Yes, it smelled bad!) From right to left: Bill Kreager, Principal Architect, Mithun; Mayor Gregory Nickels; Jennifer Potter, and Chair of the SHA board of Commissioners. Also holding a shovel is Kathy Fletcher, People for Puget Sound; Ray Hoffman, Seattle Public Utilities; and Al Doyle, Fusion Partners.

We came up with this logo, as we needed something to put on the documents being submitted to secure the entitlements from the City.

One of the pleasant surprises I encountered soon after I started at SHA was learning that I was not the only one spending a lot of free time thinking about how to respond to the challenges we faced. Another such person was Peg Staeheli, the principal at what was then SvR Design, the firm responsible for civil engineering and some of the landscaping at High Point. I fell into the habit of calling Peg on Monday mornings to ask her opinion about some decision we had made at our Friday team meeting or to see if an idea I had stewed over was possible. As often as not, Peg had also been ruminating about High Point issues over the weekend.

With the luxury of nineteen years of hindsight, it is much easier now vis-à-vis when we started in 2001 to describe the challenges facing the redevelopment effort at High Point. If I had understood the full scope and complexity of the job from the beginning, I am sure I would have been less confident jumping in. Following are several of the main challenges we faced at the start of the redevelopment:

Moving low-income families and seniors. To proceed with the redevelopment, the entire site, which housed 716 families, had to be scraped clean (except for 113 trees and the market garden), which meant that everyone had to move out of their rental homes. Moving is hard on any family, but it is an especially difficult task for families with limited incomes. (I discuss this in more detail in Chapter 4.) Although the development department would oversee the one-on-one communications with the families moving, my team had to come up with a plan that would make the dislocation as painless as possible—something easy to identify as a priority but nearly impossible to pull off.

Engaging High Point residents. High Point has been home to a diverse population for decades. Affordable SHA public housing has often served as a welcoming space for immigrants and refugees settling in Seattle, including refugees from Vietnam, Cambodia, and Laos following the Vietnam War; and from Somalia and other African nations following the armed conflicts of the 1990s.

The diversity of languages spoken at High Point reflects the diversity of the community. In 2001, the mix of languages spoken by the 620 High Point renter households was split between English and non-English speakers at 46% and 48% percent respectively, with the remaining 6% unknown.[19] Here is a breakdown of the languages spoken in the community:

[19] SHA records the ethnic diversity of people living in their properties based on language groups. Rachel Garshick Kleit and Anna Brandt, "HOPE VI for High Point: Final Evaluation Report" (June 2009), 34. Retrieved from https://cpb-us-w2.wpmucdn.com/u.osu.edu/dist/6/1264/files/2014/08/3-1rsvid2.pdf.

TABLE 2. Language Groups of High Point (2001)[20]

English	46%
East African (Amharic, Oromo, Somali, Tigrigna)	11%
Cambodian	10%
Other: Lao, Samoan, Spanish	13%
Vietnamese	19%

The site's diverse population presented unique communication challenges for the redevelopment effort. The housing authority responded to this challenge by hiring staff members from the various immigrant groups to act as interpreters and using multiple translators at community meetings.

Re-creating High Point as a safe neighborhood. The crack cocaine epidemic of the 1990s had solidified High Point's reputation, especially in West Seattle, as a dangerous place to be avoided. People who lived in High Point pointed out places where they had witnessed gunfights. People living across from the site recounted stories of seeing what appeared to be stolen household items disappearing down the street and into the community. There was a small "corner store" on the edge of the site where illegal drugs could reportedly be purchased. Parts of the site had become a dumping ground for discarded furniture and abandoned vehicles. We would be working in what was a dangerous neighborhood with the goal of creating a revitalized, safe, family-friendly community.

Addressing High Point's reputation. One of our primary goals was to create a safe neighborhood for families who would benefit from SHA's

---

[20] Does not equal 100% due to rounding

low-income housing. But if the redevelopment were to succeed, middle-income families would also have to see that the community was safe in order to want to invest in new homes there. The economic viability of the redevelopment relied on our ability to sell land to builders at a good price and, in turn, on the builders' ability to sell homes to buyers. This meant that both the crime rate and the perception of High Point as a dangerous place had to change.

Overcoming the red line in West Seattle. For years, 35th Avenue Southwest—the western border of High Point—was a dividing line for many people in West Seattle. When we started the redevelopment, there was a tacit and insidious understanding that east of 35th Avenue SW was where lower-income people lived—and maybe even were supposed to live. The area to the west of 35th was reserved for higher-income, white families.

Here is how Gary Thomsen, the Chief Sealth teacher who produced *Diaries*, described this: "Growing up there in the '50s and '60s, the common refrain among folks here was that 35th was like the Mason-Dixon Line, in that everybody who lived east of 35th was considered to be lower middle class, and those who lived west of 35th had the money, especially the closer you got to the water. And it was a line that had a pronounced influence on how families intermingled. You pretty much stayed on your side of 35th."[21]

It is possible to trace part of the history of 35th Avenue SW as a demarcation line in West Seattle to a map prepared by a federal housing agent in 1936. This map shows all of the land east of

---

[21] Gary Thomsen, email message to author, December 13, 2017.

35th in red and the land west of 35th in blue.[22] The legend on the map states that the blue section is best in the area while the red is hazardous. Although this map was prepared six years before High Point was originally built, the map shows that the area had been redlined. Redlining is a discriminatory practice that lenders never fully admitted to but that allowed the real estate industry to direct certain home buyers away from some neighborhoods and toward others. It was one of the tools that resulted in segregated neighborhoods in Seattle and communities around the country.[23]

If the redevelopment at High Point were to succeed, the price of the for-sale homes would need to be comparable to homes west of 35th Avenue SW. This would mean overcoming a sub-rosa home sale pattern in West Seattle.

Redesigning High Point's street system. Despite High Point's favorable location, the site was actually cut off from the rest of West Seattle in a number of ways. The many suburban-like curved-with-dead-end streets made it difficult to become oriented, and the street system did not connect to city streets on the perimeter. There was no way to traverse the site from north to south, and Morgan Street SW, which morphs into Sylvan SW, ran from east to west, cutting the site in two and allowing cars to speed through it. This confusing street system and the site's bad reputation meant that on-site services, such as a Seattle Public Library branch and a medical and dental clinic run by a citywide nonprofit health provider, were used primarily by High Point alone.

---

[22] Map shown in the third image at https://crosscut.com/2018/04/epic-battle-against-gentrification.
[23] Richard Rothstein, *The Color of Law* (New York: Liveright Publishing Corporation, 2017), 64.

The location of the new library (top) and clinic (bottom) within High Point, facing 35th Ave SW, signaled that the new High Point was for the whole neighborhood, not just families living within High Point, which had been the case before redevelopment.

Before SHA did anything else, it set the gears in motion to demonstrate that the new High Point would indeed be different from the old one. The decision to rebuild the library and health clinic in a new location and to make them available to both High Point neighbors as well as the public living outside of High Point signaled how substantial the changes would be.

In 1998, Seattle voters had approved a property tax levy, "Libraries for All," to build new public libraries in Seattle.[24] The Seattle library system purchased land from SHA for their new High Point library building and parking lot on the corner of 35th Avenue and Raymond Street SW, where they built a 7,200-square-foot building.[25]

SHA donated a site next to the library to the nonprofit Neighborcare, which in return built a new medical and dental clinic to serve the greater neighborhood.

The westernmost edge of the High Point site runs along 35th Avenue SW for roughly two blocks. Because 35,000 vehicles use this arterial daily, we saw it as the ideal location for a commercial center, with the library and medical clinic complementing the commercial activities.

Removing contaminants from rainwater flowing from High Point. The City of Seattle had authority over how to design the site's storm-water runoff system. Their priority was to create a drainage plan that cleaned the runoff water before it left the site to avoid further contaminating

[24] Paula Becker, "The Seattle Public Library celebrates the completion of the 'Libraries for All' capital project on September 13, 2008," HistoryLink.org, September 17, 2008, https://historylink.org/File/8773.
[25] Seattle Public Library, High Point Branch, https://www.spl.org/hours-and-locations/high-point-branch.

Longfellow Creek, a spawning ground for salmon. Our priority was to make sure the design resembled a normal Seattle street.

Eliminating the High Point/Delridge food desert. SHA's application for HOPE VI funding called for building a grocery store in the new community. As in most low-income neighborhoods, families could not get to a grocery store easily. The closest grocery store was expensive and not within walking distance, creating a food desert.[26] Was there a way to create a commercial center along 35th Avenue and recruit a grocery store to build there?

Adding density to the entire site. In order to meet our program goal of building 1,600[27] housing units on the site, the housing density would need to increase from 716 units (roughly seven units per acre) to at least fifteen units per acre. That meant the zoning would need to change. Whenever higher density is proposed, it is common for neighbors in adjacent areas to be fearful and voice their objections.

Personal Challenges

There were also the challenges I faced on a more personal level. For example, acknowledging that I was an outsider. SHA had about 600 employees at the time I went to work there. It had, and still has, a

---

[26] "Food deserts are areas that lack access to affordable fruits, vegetables, whole grains, low-fat milk, and other foods that make up the full range of a healthy diet." "A Look Inside Food Deserts," Centers for Disease Control and Prevention, last modified August 21, 2017, https://www.cdc.gov/features/fooddeserts/index.html.

[27] The final count of new units ended up at 1529; 44% are affordable rental units.

reputation nationally as a strong housing authority that gets things done. Like many in the development department, I had spent a career working elsewhere, but the rest of the SHA employees had been there for years and were more set in their outlook.

In the early 1980s, while working for King County, I found that my desire to push for quality, whether in terms of employees or services, often led to butting heads with the purchasing and human resources departments. If we were going to make High Point something special, it would take a quality effort, and I would need to figure out how to successfully navigate around the gatekeepers of those two departments.

I also had to figure out how to balance the urban planning expertise I brought to the team with my ignorance about construction. Overseeing housing and site construction contractors was to be one of my major areas of responsibility. But I knew almost nothing about how large contractors went about their work or how to work with them to build a good project. Although I would be hiring experts to monitor the contracts and there would be consultants to provide oversight, there also needed to be someone who understood how to build on budget and on time. I would have to learn on the go and tap into the skills of my team.

Integrated Design Before It Had a Name

Gary Thomsen, who was filming *Diaries,* asked if he could film one of the weekly High Point design meetings at Mithun's Seattle waterfront office. What he saw surprised him: twenty people sitting around a large conference table on a Friday morning discussing the intricacies of redevelopment planning. He had not fully grasped the scope of our work and was taken aback by how many people were involved in creating the redevelopment.

The number of people in the room was notable as it reflected the scale of the project. But there was something else far more significant going on in those two-hour meetings. The unique mix of professions at the table brainstorming and working together to develop the big picture on down to the smaller details was groundbreaking. Gary was actually observing *integrated design*, an approach that brings together design specialties that are usually managed separately. This concept was only given a label several years after these meetings took place.

I loved these Friday morning design meetings. They were where much of the magic of integrated design happened. These meetings ran weekly from mid-2001 through mid-2004, wrapping up once we were fully under construction. Brian Sullivan, the project architect, facilitated the two-hour sessions, while Peg Staeheli, the principal at SvR Design, co-directed the process. I was consulted about the agenda ahead of time, and the meetings followed a set pattern of sharing information and discussing project details.

I attended every meeting along with my core team members, the staff planner and the construction manager. Representatives from the civil engineering team, landscape architects, parks planner, and building and site planners always attended as well. Other engineers and architects participated frequently. Once we had selected a general contractor, its representative attended, too. Various experts from the design team firms—Mithun, SvR, Nakano Associates (the parks planning firm)—and other outside expert consultants were brought in to consider a wide range of topics, such as residential heating systems, streetlights, and trash collection. As the client, I was the decision-maker, so perhaps I am biased, but the meetings always felt like a collaborative process, even when there were disagreements.

Those of us leading the meetings always insisted on exploring green solutions. A green policy consultant who attended the meetings was instrumental in identifying a number of green initiatives, such as Breathe-Easy Homes (see Chapter 8). This consultant's firm also conducted the study comparing energy usage at High Point with other SHA developments (see Chapter 8).

Here are a just a few examples of how integrated design raised the bar:

■ We took a different approach to having well-lit sidewalks. We wanted to assiduously avoid the super bright prison lighting effect found in some low-income neighborhoods; at the same time, we wanted the neighborhood to be lit adequately. We looked at how to do this holistically. Our solution was to enhance the light provided by the streetlights with the porch lights on the rental units, wired so that the electrical bill was paid by management rather than the tenant. The light from the front porches allowed us to space the streetlights farther apart than usual. We also selected special street fixtures that reduced night light pollution.

■ Our approach to selecting what trees to save went beyond considering the quality and health of the trees. We looked at using trees to enhance other goals such as slowing traffic and improving small parks. We saved several trees that forced us to narrow streets with street bulbs (curbs that extend out into the normal street space). We sited rental houses further back from the standard setbacks, which had the effect of making the line of houses less ridged and more interesting. And we created a whole block with a shared backyard anchored by two large trees.

■ Managing rainwater and improving the quality of rain runoff to support an on-site salmon habitat had special significance to the project, so the design team gave it special attention. We wanted to draw attention to the downhill flow of water from the south end of the site to the pond at the north end. We started by placing birch trees—often associated with water—along the planting strips that ran in a line from the north end of the site to the pond. We reinforced the idea of a waterflow through the site by creating an artificial creek in the pond park that also served to aerate the pond water. We reinforced the watercourse by building a rain garden along this course in the Commons Park. We also placed a number of art elements, such as raindrop circles and decorated boulders, along this course.

■ Enhancing the site views of Puget Sound and the downtown skyline with a beautifully landscaped pond is such an obvious amenity that it is easy to forget that this, too, was very much an integrated design decision. We could have missed including the pond if the team had not been thinking about the whole picture from the beginning. The views from the site are exceptional, but they are even better when viewed from over the landscaped pond.

The LEED for Neighborhood Development certification[28] now requires that green projects use an integrated planning process. We did. We just called it our weekly Friday morning design meeting.

Engaged Community, Healthy Environment, Quality Design

One way to understand our unique approach to planning High Point is to explain what it was not. In another northwestern city, someone who had been a successful transportation administrator was managing a similar HOPE VI project. He set about planning and building in a lockstep fashion with tight timelines that drove all decision-making. Completing building on time was paramount.

At High Point, we had a timeline, but it was not our driving force. Our priorities were to work with the community and to enhance the redevelopment so that it resulted in a greener, healthier, well-designed community. After we had been operating for a year, I worked with a graphic designer to come up with a way to visually represent our approach, which centered on three themes: engaged community, healthy environment, and quality design (Figure 1).

---

[28] "LEED for Neighborhood Development (LEED ND) was engineered to inspire and help create better, more sustainable, well-connected neighborhoods. It looks beyond the scale of buildings to consider entire communities." "LEED certification for neighborhood development," U.S. Green Building Council, https://new.usgbc.org/leed/rating-systems/neighborhood-development.

FIGURE 1. The three themes of our approach: Engaged community, healthy environment, and quality design

Our approach was partly the result of my not knowing the "right" or traditional way to manage such a big project but trusting my management skills, which mostly meant trusting the people around me to make the right decisions. Almost everything we built was the result of a highly collaborative process. The community I engaged with included High Point residents, the integrated design team, and other colleagues in the housing authority.

For the first few years I worked on High Point, I would regularly drop by the third floor of the SHA office building to talk with housing veteran Tina Narr. At the time, Tina supervised the community builders (SHA employees working at the three HOPE VI sites whose job was to help build community among the residents), so she had a good understanding of how residents were faring as the communities underwent redevelopment.

I went to Tina because, as I started to meet the High Point neighbors, I also met with some resistance. I felt that people were holding back, that I was not getting the full story of what they were thinking. Tina told me that many people living in SHA housing had mixed feelings about people who worked at the housing authority. They had a hate-love relationship with SHA and saw SHA, above everything else, as a landlord with the ability to take away their housing.

Tina was one of many individuals working at the housing authority who provided me with information I needed to do my job well. The department esprit de corps was excellent, especially during my early years, and people shared information readily on topics I knew little about, such as affordable housing financing, management of public housing, and construction.

Sometimes information came from unexpected places. I would often stay late in my office. About an hour after everyone had left, a Somali woman—an SHA tenant who had been hired as part of the agency's employment program—would come by to do building maintenance. It turned out that she lived at High Point. We would often talk, and her conversation gave me a glimpse into the community's attitude toward the redevelopment and a vote of confidence in the work we were doing.

Many decisions were made by consensus, but there were a few design decisions I made on my own. For example, I insisted that the ceilings in all the rental units be eight and a half feet high as compared to the more standard height of eight feet. It seemed to me that adding half a foot would make the rooms feel less institutional. I also advocated putting lights in the middle of the

Commons Park. After we designed the park, I was worried that the dark middle of the park was an invitation for mischief; lights could serve as a deterrent. Additionally, I made the call that the architect's color consultant would be the final judge of the house colors. Everyone wanted a say in picking the colors, and I felt that this was one area where a compromise would not work.

Insights

Choosing an architect. Selecting the right architectural firm is very important. To do this, you need to understand the essence of your project. Given a public procurement process along with so many other considerations, this key element can get lost.

In our case, the essential piece the architectural firm Mithun brought to the table was planning and designing a master-planned community. They were skilled at designing production housing and had a history of working with developers who built master-planned communities. They had the experience to economically design hundreds of homes that also needed to be built economically and sold. That Mithun also had a strong sustainability mission was a bonus.

Small team, big results. Carrying out a big project does not take a big staff. A small number of dedicated workers can produce quality work.

CHAPTER 4

THE PROBLEM
OF RELOCATION

One of the many community meetings to explain the redevelopment plans and the rights of those living at High Point. (It was not possible, even after fourteen years, to get permission to show the faces of High Point neighbors attending this meeting.)

April 2003: I was feeling confident going into an interview with C. R. Douglas on Seattle's cable channel, Seattle Channel, which is owned by the City but acts independently. For over a year, my talking points (see Chapter 5) had been well received by both the High Point and West Seattle communities. I was accustomed to, and expected, a favorable reception. I should have seen it coming.

I was all set to talk about our plans for the new green community at High Point when, on live television, C. R. Douglas asked me something to the effect of, "Is the Seattle Housing Authority continuing its history of mistreating and displacing its low-income residents as it redevelops these large sites around Seattle?"[29] That probably was not the exact wording, but it was the gist of what I heard in the question. So much for a walk-in-the-park live TV interview.

"Well," my voice tensed up, "we have a strong program to support the residents who have to move from High Point." Chances were I would never get to my feel-good talking points. But C. R. Douglas was doing his job by asking a difficult but fair question.

At the time, the displacement of residents at the two other large Seattle HOPE VI sites was a hot topic despite the housing authority's best efforts to provide support to the families being forced to move and to tell SHA's side of the story. In general, displacement was and still is a national issue.[30] This is the Achilles' heel of HOPE VI: There is no getting around the fact

---

[29] This is the question as I remember it being asked, but it was probably worded more diplomatically. Footage of this interview, which took place in April 2003, is not available.

[30] "Criticism [of HOPE VI Projects] generally focuses on the reduction in the number of available public housing units [and] the displacement of public housing residents." Mark L. Joseph, Nancy Latham, Rachel Garshick Kleit, and Steven LaFrance, "Can San Francisco Get Mixed-Income Public Housing Redevelopment Right?" *ShelterForce*, 182 (Spring 2016): 16. Also available at https://shelterforce.org/2015/12/09/can_san_francisco_get_mixed-income_public_housing_redevelopment_right/.

that residents *are* displaced when they are forced to move from where they are living. The situation gets complicated quickly.

Displacement raises two questions. First, does the City actually "lose" permanent low-income housing units when the sites are redeveloped? Second, where do the families go when their rental homes are torn down?

Before going into the details about relocation, I need to clarify that my team was responsible to devise the plan for how the site would be divided into two phases, which would determine which families would have to move first. We were responsible for the decisions about the physical changes to the site, and our coworkers from the management staff were responsible for meeting directly with the SHA tenants on their relocation and providing one-on-one counseling.

Replacement Housing in Redevelopments

The contentious issue of replacing the low-income units in Seattle was initially aired during the discussion of NewHolly, the housing authority's first large redevelopment, in the mid-1990s. With pressure from the city council, the housing authority agreed to replace all of the torn-down units on a one-for-one basis. That is, every unit torn down would be replaced by a permanent subsidized unit with a Seattle address.

These permanent units would be either on the project site or elsewhere in Seattle.

At the time of my Seattle Channel interview, SHA had only replaced about half of the 1,352 units at both NewHolly and Rainier Vista. By 2016, however, all of the 2,068 units had been replaced for the three sites.[31] So the housing authority believes it has met the one-to-one replacement obligation.

The Appendix: Replacement Housing lists the criteria SHA uses to determine replacement housing and lists the buildings where the 716 replacement units are located.

An independent research group looked at this question of replacement housing and concluded: "SHA went farther than required (by Hope VI rules) in providing 1:1 replacement of low-income units while also providing a good mix of racial and ethnic groups."[32]

Replacement housing is more complicated than just count-ing housing units. A one-bedroom affordable housing unit is smaller than a multiple-bedroom unit and therefore cheaper to build. The city council, in reviewing the plans for High Point, wanted to make sure that the replacement units would have multiple bedrooms as was the case in the original High Point. The housing authority took responsibility for housing families

---

[31] Kerry J. Coughlin, SHA communications director, email to author, April 5, 2016.
[32] Richard Wener, Emily Alexrod, Jay Farbstein, and Robert Shibley, "Building Sustainable Neighborhoods: The 2007 Rudy Bruner Award for Urban Excellence: Silver Medal Winner: High Point Redevelopment" (Bruner Foundation, 2008), 136.

and built new affordable housing units for large families. Table 3 compares the percentage of bedrooms per unit built in the new High Point to the number of bedrooms per unit in the old High Point. In the old High Point, 42% of the units had three or more bedrooms; in the redevelopment, 60% of the units had three or more bedrooms.[33]

TABLE 3. Bedrooms per unit before and after High Point redevelopment

Bedrooms per unit	Before	After
1 BR	19%	7%
2 BR	39%	33%
3 BR	31%	52%
4 BR	11%	8%
5 BR		1%

SHA's explanation of its replacement housing program responds to criticism from the Seattle Displacement Coalition. The research team from the Bruner Foundation received the following information when their staff asked the coalition specifically about High Point:

A divergent perspective is held by John Fox of the Seattle Displacement Coalition. He argues that High Point and the other Hope VI projects have resulted in a net loss of about 1,000 affordable housing units, with High Point accounting for roughly one-third of the loss. He feels that the redevel-

---

[33] George Nemeth, Seattle Housing Authority, March 28, 2016.

opment could have been done very differently, retaining and refurbishing many of the pre-existing units, keeping more of the mature trees (he claims that only about one in six was kept), and infilling with some new, market-rate housing. … He also maintains that SHA claims units as replacement housing that would have been built anyway, and that the very substantial resources these projects absorbed were taken away from other potential projects that would have added low-cost housing.[34]

During the redevelopment, seventy-five senior units, which SHA counted as replacement housing units, were built at Providence House at High Point. Would these units have been built in Seattle anyway, as the coalition claims? It turns out that these units, which are funded by a separate HUD program, would not have been built in Seattle without a subsidy from SHA. What is also overlooked in the coalition's criticism is that SHA gave the nonprofit developers of Providence House free land, which made it possible for them to build this senior housing in Seattle.[35,36]

---

[34] Wener et al., *2007 Rudy Bruner Award*, 131–132.

[35] Because of high land prices, the HUD 202 program in Seattle works only when land is given to the nonprofit developer (as was done at all three HOPE VI sites) or when substantial other subsidies are obtained from public sources such as the City of Seattle or the State of Washington. The Low Income Housing Institute (LIHI) built several 202 projects in Seattle over the last twenty years with subsidies from outside sources.
Tim Sovold (HUD official), Robin Amadon (LIHI housing developer), and Dan Smerken (housing consultant), who worked on the three 202 projects in Seattle HOPE VI redevelopments, in conversation with author, July 11, 2016.

[36] Mr. Fox did not respond to numerous requests for additional comments about High Point in June 2016.

Housing Choice Vouchers

Housing subsidies for low-income families come in two forms. The subsidies are either connected to a specific physical housing unit, or they are given to a family who then must go into the rental housing market and find a rental unit. This second type of "floating" subsidies are called Housing Choice Vouchers (HCV) or Section 8 Vouchers. SHA received 542 HCVs for redeveloping High Point. Vouchers are not formally counted as permanent replacement housing units, because they go directly to families who use them to subsidize their apartment rent, and the voucher moves with the renter. A family that receives an HCV can take it to live almost anywhere in the country, and so many low-income families value HCVs highly. The drawback to these vouchers is that, in a tight rental market, it is hard to find an apartment with a reasonable rent. In practice, voucher holders' rental choices can be limited to less desirable locations.

Of the 542 HCVs SHA received, High Point residents who relocated out of High Point used most (76%) of these vouchers. The remaining vouchers (133) were available to families on the general SHA waiting list and were not counted as replacement housing.[37]

[37] Rachel Garshick Kleit, Sheri Reder, and Allegra Abramo, "HOPE VI for High Point Interim Report: Panel Study Baseline and Initial Relocation Outcomes," Daniel J. Evans School of Public Affairs, University of Washington (March 2004): vi–vii, https://cpb-us-w2.wpmucdn.com/u.osu.edu/dist/6/1264/files/2014/08/7-1f6d2ir.pdf.

What Happened to the Families Already Living at High Point?

My team was responsible to devise the plan for how to divide the site redevelopment into two phases. This information would direct which families would have to move first. Our coworkers from the management staff were responsible for meeting directly with the SHA tenants about the time frame and details of their relocation. This information and counseling process began a year and a half before the required moves. Moving is not particularly easy for anyone, but for residents who live in public housing, it can be a massive upheaval, as public housing offers a small piece of stability in an otherwise stress-prone environment.

Because the High Point redevelopment used federal funds, low-income neighbors living in High Point were eligible for relocation benefits. Those needing to relocate are considered the "harmed party," and the law requires that they be given plenty of notice that they will have to move.[38] The families are entitled to counseling about their housing choices, to receive moving expenses, and to receive ongoing subsidized housing. Ongoing subsidized housing takes the form of an HCV, as described earlier, and/or an opportunity to move back to the redeveloped community.

The housing authority took the position that all residents in good standing were entitled to move back to the community

---

[38] Uniform Relocation Assistance and Real Property Acquisition Act (1970).

where they formerly lived. Being in good standing meant, among other things, that the individuals were up to date with their rent and had not been cited for lease violations.

SHA's approach to screening residents returning to High Point originated with the screening practices created in the 1990s for NewHolly, SHA's first HOPE VI project. The housing authority's good standing requirements there included renters having a strong rental housing record, few late payments, a good credit rating, etc. Resident leaders at NewHolly insisted on high standards for returning residents, as the community wanted to live in a safe environment.[39] Changing High Point's reputation was integral to the redevelopment, and so SHA was in favor of policies that would reduce the risk of having disruptive renters.

"Praise Jesus!"

We had held other all-community meetings to share plans for things like street design and parks—ideas that would affect residents several years out—but this meeting would be different. Today we were showing residents where we had drawn the line between Phase I and Phase II, which meant telling them whether they would have to move in a few months or in another two years. Families who lived north of the line would have to move in the next few months (Phase I); those who lived south

---

[39] Andrew Lofton, SHA executive director, personal communication to author, July 28, 2019.

of the line could stay put for at least another two years (Phase II). Change was coming to the community for real—and soon.

As shown here, Phase I of the site was cleared by late 2004, except for legacy trees and the market garden in the north end of the site. The image also shows that grading has begun for the pond and a number of temporary ponds have been built to manage rainwater.

A large crowd showed up to the open house in the YMCA gym in the middle of High Point. I did not know what to expect, as I had not participated in similar meetings at our other redevelopments. Shortly after the doors opened, I heard a loud "Praise Jesus!" from across the gym floor. A middle-aged African-American woman was studying the map on the wall depicting the dividing line between Phase I and Phase II. She totally understood its implications for her life for the next two years, and she was ecstatic! She would not have to move immediately, and perhaps more importantly, she would not have to move twice to live in the redeveloped High Point.

The plan to divide the site in half—into Phase I and Phase II—came about because of the large size of High Point and our desire to minimize the moves some families would have to make. We would level the northern end of the site and build all of Phase I before tearing down and rebuilding the southern end of the site, which would be Phase II. We offered HCVs to anyone on the site who wanted to move off-site. This had potential to create vacancies to which families from Phase I could move into the vacant units.

There were still several challenges: First, would there be enough vacant units in the old Phase II to accommodate the residents living in the old Phase I who wanted to stay on the site during construction of the new Phase I? Second, would we have enough vacant units with the right number of bedrooms in the old Phase II to house all the Phase I families who wanted to stay? Third— and this turned out to be the biggest problem and caused major heartbreak—would the new Phase I units have the right mix of unit sizes (that is, number of bedrooms) to accommodate all the old High Point households who wanted to move back?

One heartbreaking issue we faced affected a few seniors who had lived at High Point for many years and for whom we did not have low-rise one-bedroom units (like in the old High Point) and who did not want to move into the subsidized mid-rise building in Phase I (Elizabeth House). Our relocation staff found them subsidized housing, but not in High Point.

An Independent Study of Results for Relocated Residents

Dr. Rachel Kleit, from the University of Washington (UW), led a long-term, independent study of families relocated as a result of the redevelopment. SHA provided the UW researchers with access to High Point resident files. Dr. Kleit and her colleagues interviewed residents before they moved and later attempted to track down the relocated families. An interim report from 2004 summarizes where residents went:

By May of 2003, 437, or 63 percent, of the 694 residents who were living at High Point as of the date of the HOPE VI grant (June 26, 2000) had moved away. Half (50 percent) had received a HCV. A minority (17 percent) had moved to non-HUD-assisted housing, including moving in with family, leaving the state, purchasing a home, renting locally, and a few who were unknown. Another quarter (26 percent) had moved to other SHA units, and 6 percent (or 26 households) had been evicted or had abandoned their housing units.[40]

The UW researchers interviewed households from the two large language groups, English speakers and Vietnamese speakers. The researchers intended to interview Somali speakers (the third-largest language group), but were unable to interview a non-random sample of Somali households because "these interviews took place just after the tragedy of 9/11, [and] these communities were highly suspicious of people coming to their homes to ask them questions."[41]

Kleit and team's report indicates that some families may have seen the relocation as a positive event; for example, "as an opportunity for their families, especially their children, to move away from High Point, the stigma of public housing, and drug problems they experienced there."[42] Despite this optimistic perspective, "many missed the strong sense of community and belonging they enjoyed at High Point. Moving away from High Point also caused relocatees to appreciate the services that High Point had provided, such as free garbage collection and utilities."[43]

[40] Kleit, Reder, and Abramo, "HOPE VI for High Point Interim Report," v–vi.
[41] Kleit, Reder, and Abramo, 16.
[42] Kleit, Reder, and Abramo, vi.
[43] Kleit, Reder, and Abramo, vii.

The relocatees who chose HCVs generally did so because they "were drawn to the increased housing options it provided."[44] Others opted to relocate to Scattered Site housing (SHA-owned housing throughout the city) for the continued security of living in public housing. "Most relocatees wanted to stay near High Point—usually in West Seattle. Many in the focus groups saw the move away from High Point as temporary and planned to return when the redevelopment is completed."[45]

The researchers also learned that many focus group participants were confused about the relocation process and the various rules and responsibilities pertaining to HCVs, Scattered Site housing, and related financial benefits

> Relocated residents reported receiving inconsistent and possibly incomplete information from Seattle Housing Authority (SHA). Most focus group participants were able to find housing in 2–3 months, but the experience was stressful for many of them. ... Many relocatees felt that they did not have enough choices or time, even though SHA had been informing and counseling residents for a year and a half prior to relocation. ... These sentiments, however, are not unique to High Point HOPE VI relocatees, and have been expressed by relocatees in several other cities (Smith 2002).[46]

---

[44] Kleit, Reder, and Abramo, vi.
[45] Kleit, Reder, and Abramo, vi.
[46] Kleit, Reder, and Abramo, vi, 79.

"…[O]riginal residents … elected to have those with the longest residence and who were senior or disabled have first priority for returning to the site," and the Kleit report identifies that these returning relocatee households were "the most vulnerable," as these households "were more likely to have been involved in eviction proceeding, have met local housing preferences, have received an elderly allowance, or have large families."[47] "Relocated families moved throughout the Puget Sound, with many moving to Rainier Valley and South King County, areas of relatively more racial mix and larger rental housing units. High Point relocatees in Seattle were more likely than relocatees at other sites nationally to move more than 1 mile from the original development and live in areas of low poverty."[48]

---

[47] Kleit and Brandt, iii.
[48] Kleit and Brandt, iii.

CHAPTER 5

THE WISDOM OF
THE COMMUNITY

One of the early rental housing blocks completed in Phase I.

I n the process of writing this book, I interviewed several City of Seattle officials and others involved in the redevelopment at High Point. I asked them, "What was the impact of High Point?"

Richard Conlin, a respected sixteen-year veteran Seattle City Council member, surprised me with an answer that suggested the impact had been more far-reaching than I had realized. Conlin recounted how "beat up" the city council had felt after the rezone and entitlement processes for NewHolly and Rainier Vista, the housing authority's first two major HOPE VI redevelopments. He was referring to the drawn-out and contentious hearings—separate ones for each project—that the city council had held to determine whether to give City approval to proceed with those developments.

I had attended one of these hearings for Rainier Vista. The audience—made up of Rainier Vista neighbors split 50/50 for and against redevelopment—shouted and heckled as testimony from both sides was given. Conlin told me that, because of hearings like those, if High Point had not gone so well, he was not sure that the council would have had the energy to take on the Yesler Terrace redevelopment.[49] Compared to NewHolly and Rainier Vista, High Point's entitlement process was a breeze for the city council. SHA ran a full-court press for three years in order to obtain a 9–0 vote on the rezone needed to redevelop High Point.

The significance of a 9–0 vote should not be underestimated, because it has ramifications beyond the actual approval of the

---

[49] Richard Conlin, personal communication to author, July 14, 2005.

rezone. A controversy with the rezone sets the tone for the attitude City agencies adopt toward a project, and a difficult city council review emboldens City employees who are so inclined and have the opportunity to create red tape and make the whole redevelopment process much harder. Additionally, when opponents of a project appear in front of the city council, they have the ability to extract conditions that can hamper and compromise a redevelopment effort. This had been the situation with both NewHolly and Rainier Vista, and I was determined to avoid this at High Point. It could have been a long slog not only to obtain the approval of the city council but also to work with the City to obtain all the necessary approvals to fulfill my vision for High Point. This chapter retraces the steps we took leading up to the final 9–0 city council vote in favor of the rezone.

Tapping into the Wisdom of a Community

I take the expression *tapping into the wisdom of the community* seriously, because I have seen it done successfully many times. At High Point, tapping into the wisdom of High Point neighbors and West Seattle communities was a big part of my job. We needed to listen carefully and reflect what we had heard in our planning. I devoted a large share of my time to this task during my first two years as senior project manager.

Convincing High Point neighbors and West Seattle residents that SHA could transform an area with a terrible reputation meant following former Mayor Norm Rice's advice to "Go early and go often [to the community]."[50] The geography of the place—being in the physical middle of West Seattle, a peninsula of 60,000 residents—made it easier to reach the leaders of this sizable community with our key messages. Our location meant that many of the peninsula residents would also see the changes taking place when they drove by.

I had always heard that there had been resentment in West Seattle over the original High Point development, even though it was constructed for World War II workers building planes and ships for the war effort. In late 2005, at the opening for Phase I, a nattily dressed older gentleman approached me. He was glad to see that the housing authority was finally fulfilling the promise it made in 1942 to deconstruct the temporary worker housing after the war. This gentleman represented a commonly held sentiment in West Seattle—namely, that a low-income, shoddily-built project did not belong there, and any improvement to High Point would be appreciated. That many people shared this feeling helped us to win supporters for the redevelopment.

In addition to engaging the community, we also needed to hire the best public relations consultants we could. One of the first things I did in my new role was bring in the consulting firm of PRR, a national public relations firm based in Seattle. Although

---

[50] Al Levine reported this to me soon after I was hired in June 2002.

I knew something about using visual images to help in identifying a community's values, we needed the expertise of a competent outside firm to frame and communicate our message.

The Talking Points

I had known Rita Brogan, the CEO of PRR, for twenty years and been impressed with her firm's work. When PRR came on board, I was unsure at first about how we would collaborate, but my team and I ended up working closely with Rita and her staff on multiple outreach projects. We started by creating a marketing plan, which proved to be an invaluable tool for providing the public with a consistent, positive, factual message about the redevelopment. The issue of communicating facts truthfully was important to us. "A lot of times when people put together key messages they don't pay enough attention; they just put together things they want people to believe," Rita told me. "The key messages have to be true."[51]

The Revitalization of High Point: Key Messages

The main feature of our marketing plan was a list of a dozen talking points:[52]

---

[51] Rita Brogan, personal communication to author, August 20, 2013.
[52] Seattle Housing Authority, "Talking Points for Partnership Handout," February, 5, 2003, PRR content for SHA.

1. The High Point redevelopment will knit the neighborhood back into the greater West Seattle fabric *physically* (by reconnecting the street grid), *economically* (by placing over half of the site on the Seattle tax rolls), and *socially* (by providing housing for people of all incomes).

2. High Point will be a great place to live. It will be a diverse and walkable neighborhood with sweeping views, a wide variety of high-quality housing, parks, a neighborhood commercial center, library, and a medical/dental clinic.

3. Everyone currently living at High Point will be able to return if they so choose.

4. The High Point redevelopment will result in a net increase in the Seattle Housing Authority's system of affordable housing. The number of units set aside for residents who earn less than 30% of the median income will also increase.

5. The new design brings to light many of the site's previously hidden features. The plan enhances the site's exceptional topography and allows many of the spectacular natural features to emerge.

6. The redevelopment will break down longstanding barriers between High Point and the surrounding communities. The new street grid will end High Point's physical isolation. New community facilities and parks will attract people from a wider neighborhood.

7. This is not a traditional urban renewal project where all residents are forced out. Many of the existing social connections at High Point will be retained. Approximately 320 families will stay on the site during Phase I construction, and will be the first occupants in the revitalized development.

8. Longfellow Creek will become a healthier place for salmon. Much of the creek's water comes from High Point. Because of a cutting-edge natural drainage system, High Point's storm water will now be naturally filtered before entering the creek. The filtration system will also result in more attractive green space. It will be a model for other communities.

9. SHA will develop and manage office space for small non-profit service providers as part of the redevelopment. Neighborhood House will build and operate a Head Start and Pre-Head Start facility on land provided by SHA at no cost.

10. For-sale housing built by private builders will be similar to rental housing. Rental and for-sale units will be meshed throughout the community and will be visually indistinguishable. Binding design guidelines will ensure that for-sale housing fits the wider community's look and feel.

11. The density of 1,600 units is allowed under current zoning. SHA is seeking a zoning revision in order to build some condominium buildings, and to have greater flexibility with the design and dispersion of units.

12. A private management company will run the new High Point.

I interviewed Rita in 2019 to get her perspective on these talking points. She said: "The very first message [point #1] was structured very carefully, because there were so many different kinds of stakeholders. What we needed to do was position High Point in a place where all of the stakeholders would embrace the redevelopment so they could see their individual interests reflected when we talked about the project. We helped convince a whole range of folks who would not necessarily have much to do with each other in everyday life. But their interests converged at High Point."[53]

If I am honest, it was a bit boring to deliver the same talking points again and again whenever I spoke with people about High Point, but I could tell our message was sinking in and being well received. Our outreach program, which relied heavily on these talking points, consisted of a variety of activities; for example:

Community newsletter: We mailed this annually to High Point residents and households within a mile of High Point.

Door-to-door visits or shoe-leather diplomacy: On weekends and after work, I knocked on the door of every house on High Point's perimeter (about fifty homes) to tell the residents what we were doing and to hear their concerns.

Presentations to West Seattle service clubs: I gave a presentation to every service group (Rotary, Kiwanis, etc.) I could locate in West Seattle.

Community council presentations: I attended evening meetings and gave presentations to the various neighborhood community councils near High Point. In the case of Sunrise Heights, just to the south of High Point, my presentations gave the community council a reason to meet.

West Seattle Chamber of Commerce: I joined the chamber and

---

[53] Rita Brogan, personal communication to author, May 28, 2019.

attended their monthly meetings where, for seven years, I gave an update of High Point's progress.

Large signs on the site's perimeter: In addition to the City's land-use signs, SHA put up signs about the redevelopment. The signs had my name and office telephone number, although people rarely called.

What's in a Name?

We were considering changing the High Point name, as had been done with other community redevelopments at HOPE VI sites nationally. I asked Rita for her take on this, and she shared the following reflection:

> The name *High Point* refers to the fact that the site of the community is located on a vista that is literally the high point of Seattle. But for years it had been associated with the low-income ghetto of aging structures, sociologically isolated from the rest of West Seattle. Those who did not live there had very little notion of the rich mélange of cultures inside. What they saw was shabby buildings populated by immigrants. What they thought was they should avoid even driving through, because it felt dangerous.
>
> In considering what to call this new, economically integrated development, the immediate reaction was to come up with a

shiny new name that would break from the old High Point brand, eradicating the memory of the place that was. The new community would be woven into the larger West Seattle neighborhood. It would include both renters and homeowners. And it would be beautiful. Children from lower-income families would play in parks side by side with children from middle-income families. This economic integration would help them see themselves not as "the other," but as part of a diverse and integrated place. And those in the market-rate homes would have an opportunity to get to know families different from themselves.

So what could be a better name than High Point? In addition to being a literal description of the community's elevation, the name also connotes the aspiration of this new community. The name stuck.[54]

High Point was here to stay.

Visual Surveys

A favorite technique of ours was using visual images to solicit ideas from the community. Although we would have used photographs anyway to learn what people wanted to see in the new High Point regardless of the community demographics, the added bonus of doing this was that it made it possible for non-English speakers

---

[54] Rita Brogan, personal communication to author, May 22, 2019.

to provide their preferences. Showing residents and neighbors images of what might be built at High Point gave them a voice. For example, we showed a variety of houses to find out people's preferences for key design features such as front porches, garages facing the street, house colors, window sizes, pitched roofs, and styles (modern, craftsman, etc.). We used the images in a variety of settings over several months and discovered some consistent findings, which we passed on to the designers of the affordable housing and used to prepare design guidelines for the for-sale homes.

As time went by, we continued to expand our methods for tapping into the wisdom of the community when it came to design details of the new High Point. We wanted residents and neighbors to know that their input mattered in this endeavor. In addition to the visual surveys, we also did the following:

High Point Diversity Festival: We helped to keep this annual summer festival alive after the redevelopment started. We put up boards at our booth with large images of housing styles so festivalgoers could give us feedback on which housing style was appropriate for the new High Point.

Community newsletter: We dedicated one of our community newsletters to obtaining neighborhood preferences for various residential design approaches. We mailed a few thousand of these newsletters and received a strong response. I am embarrassed to say that, for some reason, no one counted the number of replies; however, several of us remember a stack of responses about six inches high, held together by a large rubber band.

An example of one of the newsletters we mailed to a wide audience living in or close to High Point.

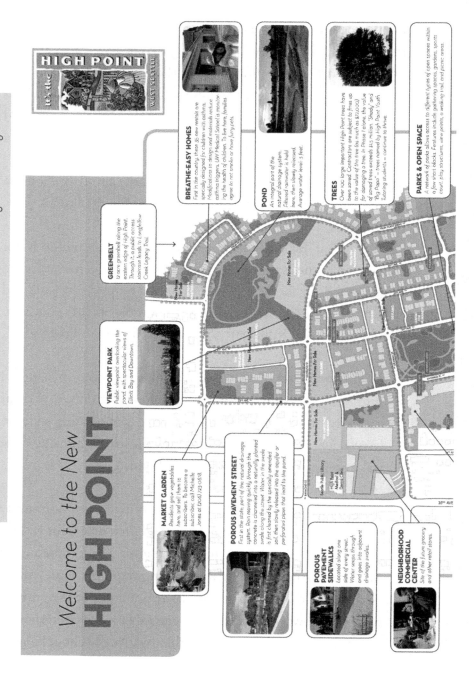

Welcome to the New
HIGH POINT

GREENBELT
Izrace greenbelt along the eastern edge of High Point. Through it, a public access staircase leads to Longfellow Creek Legacy Trail.

VIEWPOINT PARK
Public viewpoint overlooking the pond with spectacular views of Elliott Bay and Downtown.

MARKET GARDEN
Residents grow vegetables here, and sell them to subscribers. To become a subscriber, call Michelle Jones at (206) 725-0518.

POROUS PAVEMENT STREET
First in the state, part of the natural drainage system. Rain moving quickly through the concrete is channeled into a naturally planted swale along the street. Water in the swale is first cleaned by the specially amended soil, then slowly released into the aquifer or perforated pipes that lead to the pond.

POROUS PAVEMENT SIDEWALKS
Located along one side of every street. Water seeps through and goes into adjacent drainage swales.

NEIGHBORHOOD COMMERCIAL CENTER
Site of the future grocery and other retail stores.

BREATHE-EASY HOMES
First in the country, these 36 new rentals are specially designed for children with asthma. Modifications to design and materials reduce asthma triggers. UW Medical School is monitoring the health of children. To live here, families agree to not smoke or have furry pets.

POND
An integral part of the natural drainage system. Filtered rainwater is held here, then slowly released. Average water level: 5 feet.

TREES
Over 100 large important High Point trees have been saved. Contractors are subject to fines up to the value of the tree (as much as $20,000) for damaging a tree. In those I drove, the value of saved trees exceeds $1.5 million. "Shady" and "Big Papa" – trees named by High Point Youth tutoring students – continue to thrive.

PARKS & OPEN SPACE
A network of parks allows access to different types of open spaces within a few short blocks. Features include gathering spaces, gardens, sports court, play structures, view points, a walking trail, and picnic areas.

PHASE II OF HIGH POINT

Deconstruction and demolition to be completed by July 2003, followed by roads and under-ground infrastructure construction. Morgan/Sylvan Way SW to be made into a boulevard. Building construction begins Summer 2003.

LONGFELLOW CREEK

Nearly all of High Point's drainage flows into this rare urban creek. Ongoing High Point's natural drainage system) are designed to protect habitat. New trail system links creek to the community and provides recreation opportunities.

PHASE II
(2006 – 2009)

Phase II Homes For Sale

DECONSTRUCTION

Old houses dismantled one board at a time, saving wood and other materials, helps create jobs and reduces landfill material.

RENTAL TOWNHOMES

"Big house-look," variety of designs, bright colors - as requested by High Point residents.

POCKET PARKS

Found on nearly all rental blocks, ideal places for small children to play, or to have a block party.

SWALES

Shallow planting strips, covered with grass or native drought-tolerant plants. Below, topsoil and mixture cleans water. Deep containments, perforated pipes carry overflow to pond.

ELIZABETH HOUSE SENIOR LIVING

75-unit, independent living, low-income senior apartment building, owned and operated by Sisters of Providence. Opens January 2006.

SENIOR RETIREMENT BUILDING

140-unit, independent living, market rate apartment building. Services include three meals a day. Construction begins Spring 2006.

ART INSTALLATIONS

A series of art elements, designed by former West Seattle resident Bruce Myers, tell the story of the Longfellow Creek watershed and the rainwater cycle. The native birch tree, in stainless steel or ca sculpture, boulders sandblasted with images of insects, bronze manhole covers with images of fish, rain drops and waves in curb cuts and mounted on light poles, raindrop patterns scored into the pavement, and splash blocks from roof downspouts - all these are reminders for us to be responsible guardians of our fragile habitat.

Bringing Healthy Innovations Home

A lot of attention is now being focused on positive life-style changes that reduce the incidence of, and suffering from, the near-epidemic of childhood and adult asthma.

To address this pressing health issue, Seattle Housing's High Point Team collaborated with the University of Washington, the King County Health Department, and the American Lung Association of Washington to implement a long-range program designed to improve indoor air quality, and ultimately reduce the occurrence of asthma attacks in children.

Through the program, 35 innovative Breathe-Easy Homes have been designed and built for rent to qualified low-income families. These homes incorporate special features to reduce indoor air pollutants and increase the quality of life for the residents.

The residents of the homes were chosen on the basis of surveys assessing the severity of their children's asthma. Once accepted into the program, residents completed a questionnaire that will serve as a baseline for monitoring.

Specialists then visit the participant's current homes and, as much as possible, improve the air quality by removing home environmental pollutants and educating the families. The families are then given a second questionnaire as they leave their old home for their new one at High Point. A final questionnaire will be presented to them after they have lived in their new High Point home for 12 months.

Each of the program's participants must follow a sensible list of rules to ensure the highest possible air quality for the children. These include no smoking, no furry pets, and a restriction on using certain cleaning agents.

The Breathe-Easy Homes include a variety of features, including:

- An air filtration system in the homes' attics to filter and remove stale air.
- A hydronic heating system to reduce airborne particles and organisms.
- Linoleum flooring and window blinds that diminish dust from collecting in carpets and curtains.
- Low-VOC (volatile organic compounds) paints and cabinetry to reduce potentially harmful off-gas emissions.
- Airtight wall construction, insulated windows, and insulated foundations to minimize dust, pollen, and other containments, which can enter from outside.
- A HEPA filter vacuum cleaner that efficiently removes dust and other toxins or debris.

The High Point Fair: In March 2004, several hundred people attended a fair at the High Point Elementary School, on the southern edge of the community. We put on this fair, in part, as a way to model our number-one talking point—knitting the neighborhood back into the greater West Seattle fabric. The fair was a fun event for both High Point residents and our surrounding neighbors, with food and entertainment provided, and various ways for those attending to learn more about our plans. We solicited information from fairgoers by requesting their participation in a dot exercise where people put dots on the house style they felt was appropriate for the new community.

A High Point neighbor expresses his choice for the style of house he would find appropriate for the new community.

Raise Your Hand exercise: In order to solicit opinions from many of High Point's immigrant neighbors, we had to navigate the language barrier. With the permission of the resident council, we held separate meetings with immigrant groups and an interpreter. Our large all-community meetings could be chaotic as they required multiple interpreters speaking into a closed circuit intercom system, which meant that the attending residents needed headsets. Participants had a better opportunity to be heard at the smaller meetings. They "voted" for the image they preferred and expressed their opinions about why they liked it.

The design information we obtained from all of our visual preference work went into the designs of both the rental houses and the design guidelines we required the for-sale homebuilders to follow. We found that people living in West Seattle (that is, within High Point and the area surrounding the neighborhood) preferred a traditional craftsman housing style. They wanted buildings to look like big houses with large windows, front porches, and a modulated façade. This was the opposite of the barrack-like, plain buildings found at the old High Point. People liked houses that had bright colors and did not want visible garages in the front of homes.

Other Forms of Community Outreach

Reaching out to solicit opinions from people and—importantly—actually listening to what they said seemed to ease people's anxiety about the upcoming changes. The understandable anxiety that is often part of any change was replaced by factual information and personal relationships, as SHA staff interacted regularly with people in the community. The venues for these encounters ranged from people's living rooms, to meeting rooms on the site, to outdoor events.

Important conversations about design details other than housing styles emerged from these meetings as well. For example, early in the process we showed drawings of the proposed new pond to the residents at a community meeting. One East African woman had questions about the use of the water. We first needed to explain that, due to Seattle's climate and geography, it was okay to not turn all held water into drinking water. Her next concern was for the water safety of children in the neighborhood. My initial thought was, *There are no fences around the lakes in Seattle. Why do we need a fence around a three-foot-deep pond?* But I put my first reaction aside and listened some more. I realized that water safety skills are an important issue to newcomer families who have not grown up around bodies of water. After checking with the engineers, we came up with a way to build the fence without penetrating the plastic membrane that lines the pond. A three-foot fence surrounds the pond today.

Gaining community input was an ongoing project, and we used a variety of approaches to engage the community:

Resident Information Center (RIC): After the dust had settled from the demolition of rental units in Phase I in the summer of 2004 as well as the relocation of many of the residents, there were still a few empty rental units on the site. We turned one of these into the RIC. We held our weekly on-site meetings in the unit, as it was convenient for residents who occasionally attended the meetings. We stored our outreach material there and occasionally held small open houses for residents to learn more about the redevelopment plans. We also set aside a separate empty unit as an office for the resident council's use.

Small hands-on design committee: At one point, we needed advice on some basic design questions, such as the color and texture of the carpet and the color of the countertops. We organized a small committee of English speakers to advise us. For several Saturdays we met, took off our shoes, and walked on different carpets to feel what they were like; then we looked over samples. The group enjoyed the process and appreciated being involved, and we found consensus for the choices we ended up using.

Initial Art: During the High Point 2004 fair, Milenko Matanovic from the Pomegranate Center ran a hands-on exercise he called *Initial Art*. Milenko and team encouraged fairgoers to grab a brush and paint a slate for the new wooden fence being built around the site's market garden (a large half-acre garden at the northwest corner of the site that was kept intact and improved as part of the redevelopment). We then nailed all the painted slates on to the fence, where they are to this day. This fence gives people like me and other neighbors something personal to look for when visiting the community.

These are the fence slats (initial art) created at the High Point Fair and placed around the market garden.

Birds of the world: Another area where we sought input was for the woodcarvings that make up the backdrop for the amphitheater built in the redevelopment. I turned this over to Milenko. We asked the teachers of the Muslim Saturday morning class to bring their students, about 75 eight- to fifteen-year-olds, to the school gym, where Milenko conducted a brainstorming session. After about fifteen minutes, the group decided that, because of the diversity in the community, birds from around the world should be the theme of the woodcarvings. Over the next several weeks Milenko recruited residents, and they carved the wood panels.

High Point students recommended that the amphitheater have carvings of birds from around the world. Here's an example.

The Stakeholders Group

We decided early on to go big with the stakeholders group. Instead of selecting a small group of leaders to represent all of West Seattle, we cast our net wide and invited fifty-four people to join the Partnership for High Point's Future. The group included leaders from nearly every civic group in West Seattle, leaders from nearby neighborhood councils, real estate professionals, and education and health leaders. We invited High Point resident council members as well as business owners in the High Point neighborhood.

The author giving a presentation to a meeting of the Partnership for High Point's Future.

From this large group, we let people self-select. Those interested came to a meeting every three months in 2002 and early 2003. During this time, we made all of the design decisions and used the partnership as our sounding board. We gave carefully planned presentations in tightly managed meetings with agendas that had been mailed out in advance. We sent minutes and meeting materials to the whole partnership so that those who did not come to the meeting (and the free lunch we provided) could still get a good idea of what we were working on.

While there were a few occasions when one or two specific individuals objected to something we presented, the conversation was always civil and respectful, albeit intense. Only a map showing the location of the rental and the for-sale housing drew nearly unanimous objections from the members. The group strongly objected to a plan that had homeowners living almost exclusively on the perimeter of the site on blocks with the best views. We modified this arrangement and, at the next meeting, showed the members the more integrated plan we ended up using.

The care and nurturing of this partnership paid off in many ways. We created a positive buzz in the neighborhood, and I am pretty sure that some of this was the result of committee members reporting back to their organizations. We asked committee members to testify at the High Point city council public hearing, and sixteen did. Two members also provided testimony before the Seattle Hearing Examiner who reviewed and ultimately approved our plan.

Building for Residents, Not Architects

The city council had scheduled this one public hearing at High Point as part of its review of the contract rezone for the High Point redevelopment. The housing authority had submitted an application to the City that called for doubling the density at High Point from roughly seven to fifteen units per acre. On this evening, Lavonne Conquest and other High Point residents and neighbors had a chance to express their views publicly.

What would Ms. Conquest say in her testimony at the public hearing at High Point on the evening of April 29, 2003? She was a respected resident with a reputation for speaking her mind, and that made me nervous. Her comments would carry a great deal of weight.

There were twenty-seven speakers that evening at the High Point elementary school gym. Lavonne was one of the last speakers. Up to that point, the comments by various neighbors and service providers had been positive. Then Lavonne got up to speak. Here's part of what she said: "They are not building this for housing [SHA] or for the architects; they're building this for those of us who live at High Point."[55]

Much to my surprise and great relief, there was no negative testimony from anyone that night. Our outreach strategies had worked so well that, early in the council deliberations, council member Nick

---

[55] Lavonne Conquest, Seattle City Council public hearing, April 29, 2003.

Licata, a longtime critic of SHA's redevelopment efforts, praised the redevelopment by saying that the new High Point would "weave the new community into the fabric of West Seattle."[56] Here was a council member espousing one of our talking points! Our outreach efforts had succeeded far beyond our expectations.

The final city council vote was—you guessed it, unanimous: 9–0.

Insights

Authentic conversation. All of our efforts to reach out to residents and neighbors worked only because we were sincerely interested in hearing what people had to say. That does not mean we did everything people wanted, but where we could, we did include their ideas. We built in feedback mechanisms along the way that demonstrated that we were listening and making the changes we could based on what people told us. It took a long time, but by providing consistent, honest answers, we built trust between us and High Point and West Seattle residents and neighbors. I probably should not have been so worried when Lavonne got up to speak.

Invest in communication. We spent $25,000 on the development and implementation of our marketing plan. Was it worth the money? We were able to start construction on the

---

[56] Seattle City Council chambers, May 27, 2003.

$50 million Phase I infrastructure and affordable housing right away once we received the council's approval. Any controversy would have delayed this approval, as had happened at our other two projects. One month's delay with a 9.5% construction cost inflation[57] increases the cost by $39,500 per month. It is easy to calculate that, yes, this was a cost-effective investment.

Learning from diversity. The East African woman who asked for a fence around the pond was right about the danger. A few years ago, a three-year-old somehow found a way around the fence and had to be rescued from the water.

---

[57] Turner Building Cost Index, 2005.

PART 3
GREENING
THE COMMUNITY

CHAPTER 6

THE NATURAL DRAINAGE SYSTEM

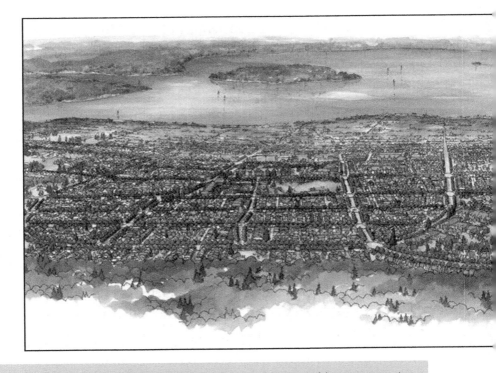

Before anything new was built, we hired an artist to create a vision of the new community. The painter took some liberties by turning the site into a waterfront property (not really the case) in this view of High Point looking west at Puget Sound. The drawing illustrates how High Point streets connect with surrounding streets.

From the City's perspective, High Point presented a straightforward but tantalizing opportunity to take advantage of a major land-use change in order to better manage rainwater on-site and improve the water quality in Longfellow Creek. For the SHA development team, this introduced a new challenge: what to do, given financial and bureaucratic restraints, to create a traditional-looking Seattle neighborhood that met the City's surface water quality requirements and also treated rainwater as efficiently as a mountain meadow. Our solution—building a natural drainage system—turned out to be the linchpin for our subsequent green approach at High Point.

It is worth noting that building green was not part of SHA's application for $38 million to HUD in May 2000. Although the draft site design was based on New Urbanist ideas, there were only two references in the application that hinted at incorporating green features into the High Point redevelopment: 1) consideration of an on-site storm-water management program, and 2) a mention of the need for healthy indoor air.

The world has changed since we started planning High Point in 2001, and being green is now much more widely accepted. But during most of the planning and building phases, SHA used the term *healthy* rather than *green*. We did this for two reasons. First, focusing on building *green* by itself could have, in some ways, pigeonholed our broader concerns, which included how the environment affected the health of low-income residents. Second, as hard as it is to believe now, in 2001, *green* was not a mainstream development pattern, and our agency preferred to act with caution.

A number of factors converged to result in our creating an integrated green redevelopment—which, in hindsight, appears to have been a carefully orchestrated effort. It is not as though we fell into this result. It took some thought and effort, of course, but at the same time, my boss was skeptical about incorporating green elements in our plans. Other SHA leaders were cautious, too, but to their credit, they never told me *not* to go green. Our inadvertent strategy, at least initially, was to piecemeal our green initiatives, and this ended up being an effective way to slip under the radar what was about to happen on this 120-acre site in West Seattle.

The Deal with the City of Seattle

Soon after taking on the position of senior development manager in 2001, I started hearing the term *natural drainage system* (NDS; see figure 2), which referred to a new way to accommodate rainwater. I had no idea what this system actually was, but I was told that the City wanted to install one at High Point, and that there was a completed demonstration project in the north end of Seattle called the Street Edge Alternatives (SEA) Project. I had also heard that the City might actually mandate building an NDS at High Point.

FIGURE 2. Two streets with a natural drainage system: High Point on the top *(typical High Point street built like a traditional Seattle street with on-street parking on both sides and a wide planting strip)* and the low-density site in North Seattle on the bottom.

So I went out and looked at the SEA streets in North Seattle, and I became worried. The City had constructed a relatively narrow, curvy street with wide swales, no curb, and no on-street parking. Although this street design fit in with the lower-density, more rural feeling of that North Seattle neighborhood, there were big problems with using this newly rebuilt street as a model for High Point. The first was that this snaking street did not look like any other I had ever seen, and I was a firm believer in what the king of New Urbanism, Andrés Duany, had to say on the subject. His position is that architects should never conduct design experiments with affordable housing neighborhoods; they should look like middle-class neighborhoods.[58]

Another problem with the SEA design solution was that it did not look like it could withstand the natural wear and tear of the more than 1,200 children who would be living at High Point. SHA intended to build units with multiple bedrooms, because we wanted to serve large families. It was not an exaggeration to expect that, in good weather, High Point would be teeming with children playing outside. Grass-covered front yards and planting strips would withstand heavy use much better than areas with the low plants and bushes used in the SEA street design.

Our initial concern was compounded a month later when we heard that the State of Washington had given the City final

[58] Andrés Duany Lecture, Suburban Sprawl, YouTube video, August 27, 2012, https://www.youtube.com/watch?v=NMvwHDFVpCE.

authority to approve the drainage plan for High Point. SHA's most recent experience at the Rainier Vista redevelopment was fresh in our minds. The City had required us to build to a street standard we did not want: 28-feet-wide streets with parking on one side only. We had wanted narrower streets with parking on both sides. However, fire departments almost always lobby for wider streets, because, they argue, wider streets are easier for fire trucks to maneuver.

In addition, we knew from the outset that the City staff working on drainage issues saw the redevelopment at High Point as a great opportunity to do something about rainwater flow, because of High Point's size and location and the direction water flowed off its 120 acres. These 120 acres are the source of about eight percent of the rainwater that flows into the important salmon-bearing Longfellow Creek.

Historically, Longfellow Creek had contained populations of coho salmon, cutthroat trout, and steelhead trout. However, in 1999, when the City's surface water utility, Seattle Public Utilities (SPU), conducted spawning surveys on the creek, it recorded only sixty adult coho salmon. SPU scientists determined that the biggest problem for salmon in urban streams came from poor-quality rainwater flowing into the stream, following even a minor storm, rather than the suitability of the streambed itself. Redeveloping High Point was a once-in-a-generation opportunity to do something about the quality and quantity of rainwater that flowed into Longfellow Creek.

It was in this context that our design team met and worked out what we could request from the City in return for giving them the water quality and flow they wanted from the High Point site. Our list had four items:

1. Twenty-five-feet-wide streets with parking on both sides on all our internal streets.
2. A streetscape design that looked like a regular city street.
3. Funding for the additional cost of building an NDS.
4. A commitment from the City for expedited approvals to build the community.

Our team had several meetings with the City's representatives to review what each party wanted. Ray Hoffman, a tall, wiry man with a ponytail, led the City's team. Ray was a special assistant to the SPU director. He arrived a little late to our first morning meeting, bicycle helmet under his arm.

I paid particular attention to Ray. Who was this unconventional man who was clearly running the show? He seemed to be assessing our team, perhaps wondering whether we were committed and competent enough to deliver. It seemed to me that he was thinking, "I'm sticking my neck out for these guys. Is that a good idea?"

We took small steps toward making a deal, each of us feeling the other side out. Because Ray was discreet about the information he shared with us, we knew he would be discreet with the information we provided him. There were other City departments that could be counted on to object to elements of what we were asking, so our proposal had to be kept quiet. I learned later on that Ray had worked astutely with the mayor's office to neutralize the fire department's complaint about the planned twenty-five-feet-wide streets.[59]

Because the interests of the two agencies lined up, in the end, there was little bickering over the contents of the deal. In exchange for building an NDS, the City supported us in obtaining the necessary permits to build the New Urbanist site plan we wanted for High Point. Subsequent meetings focused mostly on working out the mechanics that provided SPU with the assurance they needed that we would build the drainage system as promised (including honoring the agreed-upon amount of impervious surface[60] on each High Point block), the schedule for obtaining city council approval for building the NDS, and details on other issues, such as the reimbursement schedule for the extra cost of building the NDS.

Additionally, there was one specific power given to SHA as part of the expedited permit approval process that made the implementation of the NDS possible. We were not pre-

---

[59] We made several upgrades to increase safety on the site, including putting automatic sprinklers in nearly all of the rental housing and placing the fire hydrants in easy-to-access locations.
[60] On every block—and it varied by block depending on its location—we had to limit the amount of surface that prevented rainwater from soaking into the ground. This was done using a variety of techniques, including covering parking spaces with gravel, using porous pavement sidewalks, and building wide planting strips.

sumptuous enough to ask for this, but Ray understood the special challenges we faced and provided for them. When SHA encountered an individual who was reluctant to look at the existing rules with the fresh perspective required to build the NDS, we could request that that individual be temporarily moved from their assignment. We used this authority, very quietly, eight times.

To dispel any impression that we operated like characters in *The Godfather*, I will give an example. A plans examiner held up a building permit on a particular block because the buildings and the alley were configured in such a way that water would sheet flow across the alley. *Sheet flow* refers to water spreading across a surface rather than flowing through a channel. Sheet flow is not allowed in a conventional drainage system, but it was a necessary component of the natural drainage system we were building. Nonetheless, the examiner insisted that he could not approve this instance of sheet flow. So we arranged for another planner to approve the design rather than wait weeks for a resolution.

As is often the case, people working at my level (several steps down from the executive director) are the ones who set the tone for important negotiations. Recently, I interviewed my City counterpart Miranda Maupin, who led the City's efforts to build the natural drainage system at High Point. I asked for her perspective on how we were able to build the country's largest NDS. She responded with one word: "Trust." And she is right. There were reams of paper codifying our agreement, but in the end it boiled down to the two sides trusting each other. The end result of this partnership was probably the most innovative, most important thing we accomplished at High Point. Or, to put it another way, it was our contribution to the world: a natural drainage system that looked like a regular old Seattle street.

The Natural Drainage System and the Pond

High Point's pond with rental housing in the background.

FIGURE 3. A High Point streetscape shows how the High Point drainage system works to recharge groundwater and protect Longfellow Creek.

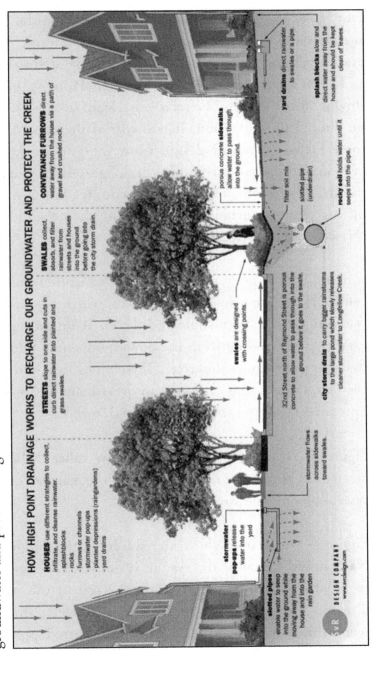

Our goal in designing the High Point natural drainage system was to simulate a mountain meadow. That is, despite all the streets, sidewalks, planting strips, homes, and driveways, rainwater leaving High Point would flow slowly off the site and be relatively clean, because it would be filtered by vegetation. It was within the constraints of these factors that our design team went to work to not only create the largest natural drainage system (Figure 3) that had been built to date in the country but also pull it off successfully without compromising the neo-traditional (New Urbanist) streetscape.

A natural drainage system is a radical departure from a conventional catch basin and pipe system, which captures rainwater as quickly as possible and directs it into a pipe. The smaller pipes leading from the downspouts on a house lead to larger pipes under the street. These pipes are connected to even larger ones that can carry an overwhelming amount of untreated rainwater into a creek, pond, or lake.

Figure 3, created by SvR Design (now called MIG), was created to show the many pieces of the natural drainage system on any one street.

Figure 3 summarizes how the water in the High Point NDS flows. Much of the system is designed for rainwater to be absorbed into the ground. The rest of the water is directed into swales on one side of the street; the water seeps through a special soil mix into slotted pipes that then send water to the pond, which slowly releases water into Longfellow Creek. There is a delicate balance between slowing the water and letting it flow freely through the swales. The dirt in the swales is a combination of gravel and compost that, along with various plantings, cleans and holds the rainwater for up to twenty-four hours so that it does not overwhelm the pond.

Had it not been for these less visible features of the natural drainage system, we would have had to build a pond that was roughly five times larger than the one that exists at High Point today. The size of the pond was an important factor from the beginning, because a larger pond would have severely limited the space available to build the number of housing units we needed to meet our low-income housing goals. This in turn would have reduced potential income from selling land to private builders, which we also needed to make our budget whole. There was never any question that we had to limit the size of the pond to roughly three and a half acres and thus find other ways to "naturally" account for all of the rainwater that fell on the site.[61]

Most of the time, the water level in the High Point pond is only three feet deep. However, the pond can accommodate a great deal more water (for example, from a storm) and rise another ten feet to a large drain that is much like the overflow drain in a bathtub. The water in the pond drains

---

[61] Seattle's average annual rainfall is 37.49 inches. "Rain Stats," Seattle Weather Blog, last modified 2017, http://www.seattleweatherblog.com/rain-stats.

through a small pipe to Longfellow Creek. During a minor storm, water continues to drain in slowly as the pond level increases. In a major storm, more water is released into the creek, where it combines with other rainwater. The creek then reaches very high levels, but this is a natural phenomenon that does not affect the salmon habitat.

Building Green Challenges: Swales and Pervious Concrete

A few of the green infrastructure elements created problems for us. The first involved the swales on one side of every street. Peg Staeheli led the charge to get the contractors to think about the swales in an entirely nontraditional way—not an easy task. The swales, which clean the water flowing through them, had to be thought of as part of a drainage system, as important as any pipe in the system. That meant that the landscaped swales needed to be built early in the process and not put off to the end, which traditionally is when landscaping is put in. This was a hard concept to get across, as was the idea that the soil in the swales had to be kept in good condition and not be contaminated by silt from the road. Essentially, small dams had to be built to block the dirty street water from flowing through the cuts that had been made in the curbs. Every member of the contractor's crew had to understand that they could not shovel dirt from the street into the swales when it came time to clean up the site.

Installing porous concrete also caused some problems. These days there are companies that specialize in this product. They have crew members who know that using this special cement

Here the temporary soil covering a perforated pipe (with holes to collect water, at the bottom of the swale) is being removed to be replaced by bioretentive soil. Grass and drought-resistant plants will be planted on top of the swale. During construction, heavy equipment ran using biofuel.

correctly means following a set of steps that are entirely different from putting in traditional concrete. For one thing, when cement is initially poured, it has to be covered with plastic and cannot be smoothed over to look just right.

The sidewalk contractor in Phase II had been working with concrete for many years and did not take the time to train his crew on how to install the porous concrete correctly. As a result, the crew had to return to the job site and break up the concrete they had installed incorrectly and redo their work at various places across the site.

Success

Most of the drainage elements that make the NDS at High Point so successful are subtle. The streets look perfectly normal, although in fact they are slanted slightly in one direction rather than bowed in the middle like regular streets. The slant allows water to flow into curb cuts every fifteen feet or so and then into the swales. There is a dry side and a wet side to each street. The wet side has the swale and a porous pavement sidewalk that allows the water to flow through it into the ground. In another effort to make the streetscape look as regular as possible, the swales adjacent to the rental housing, where the majority of the children in the community live, are covered with grass rather than shrubs.

FIGURE 4. Top: Over time the vegetation in the swales has matured and become an important green feature of the community. Bottom: Another example of matured vegetation in the swale.

The relatively narrow streets (25 feet wide with parking on both sides), the wide planting strips (half with swales), and the sidewalks all combine to make a very walkable neighborhood. Additionally, the trees and other vegetation planted in the strips took off in the amended soil, allowing the community to have a healthy tree canopy in record time.

Prior to High Point, most residential natural drainage systems hid the swales, but in the High Point streetscape design, the swales actually enhance the community as they separate pedestrians on the sidewalk from the moving cars on the street. Having parking on both sides of the street makes for an even safer environment for pedestrians.

There is also a quarter-mile walking trail that surrounds the pond and is used heavily by High Point residents and neighbors. Elsewhere in the country there are subdivisions with ponds hidden in a remote corner and surrounded by a chain-link fence topped with barbed wire. At High Point the short three-foot fence encircling the pond provides safety for young children, but the fence is not so high that it keeps teenagers from playing on it during the rare freeze when it becomes a giant skating rink.

More importantly, the NDS not only looks good but it also cleans the rainwater. Today, the Open Space Association under Janelle Gonyea maintains the NDS, including the pond, which the association empties annually. Janelle confirms that the system works and that "most of the contaminants are being removed through the series of grasses and bio-retention soil."[62]

---

[62] Janelle Gonyea, personal communication to author, January 2019.

The NDS, with its pond and the swales, had potential to be a major liability for High Point. Instead, we turned it into an asset.

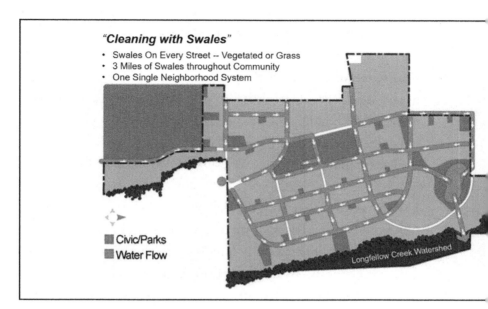

"Cleaning with Swales"
- Swales On Every Street -- Vegetated or Grass
- 3 Miles of Swales throughout Community
- One Single Neighborhood System

■ Civic/Parks
■ Water Flow

Longfellow Creek Watershed

The rainwater that falls on the site is either absorbed into the ground or channeled through pipes to the pond.

Insights

Rely on the experts. The solution to High Point's drainage system reflects the specific conditions found on the site, particularly its location atop a hill. We wanted rainwater to soak into the ground, but we needed to control the amount. The size of the pipes and of the pond also reflect the climate in Seattle. Every application of a natural drainage system concept should reflect local conditions. That said, if it is feasible to treat rainwater in a visible manner using the streetscape, like we did, by all means do it. People appreciate being able to see the system that treats their rainwater.

Clarify wants in negotiations. Make it something the other side has the capacity to deliver. All four of the things we insisted upon in exchange for building the natural drainage system required the City to be flexible and change some of the ways they operated, but with sufficient political will, they were able to deliver on all four items.

Use discretion. Reaching the deal with the City required discretion from both parties. Our meetings took place in the upper-floor offices of the municipal office building, which required taking two different elevators. Because our team could not be sure who else might be sharing the elevator, we adopted a rule never to discuss what had happened in the meeting on the way down.

Pick the right partner. Not only did SPU benefit from strong leadership in the person of Ray Hoffman (who eventually became their director), but the organization was well managed and had a good relationship with the mayor and the city council.

Choose your brand carefully. I am not sure where the term *natural drainage system* came from, but it works. Although marketers overuse the word *natural,* in this case, the name does reflect a design that relies on the soil to clean contaminants in rainwater. People have responded positively to living on a street that is part of a natural drainage system.

CHAPTER 7

STREETS AND TREES

MIG/SvR, Above the Rest Photography

After extensive negotiations, Sylvan/Morgan (shown here) was built as a two-lane boulevard with a turning lane and streetlight at the corner of Lanham Pl SW. This narrower street slows traffic and reduces the separation between north and south High Point.

One of the big issues we needed to resolve was how to create a street network that knit High Point into West Seattle. As was the standard practice, SHA would build the streets at High Point and then turn them over to the City of Seattle, who would own and maintain them. The street design needed to be a collaborative effort, and this process began with a meeting at High Point between the key City road planners and our design team. The meeting went well for us, as the City road planners agreed with the street pattern we wanted.

I assumed that Peg, who led this meeting, had used some magic formula to ensure that the outcome would be to our liking. I later heard that she had done something unusual when it came to arranging who would sit together. At first, I pictured something complicated, like organizing wedding party seating, but when I finally had the chance to ask her what she had done, I was impressed with the elegant simplicity of her answer. Peg had used an approach she had seen work effectively in a middle-school classroom: She divided the attendants into two groups with all the outgoing, vocal people at one set of tables and the quieter, more reticent participants at another set of tables. That was it. No magic involved. It was her way of making sure all the attendants had a voice.

The major breakthrough at this meeting was the decision to create a street that traversed the site from north to south, effectively connecting High Point's street grid to neighboring streets. This was a big deal in terms of how High Point was integrated with, rather than isolated from, the rest of West Seattle. It was a major change from the spaghetti-like street pattern that had existed at High Point since the early 1940s, and it aligned the streets with the site's terrain. In addition, the streets were configured so that streets on the site's perimeter now connected across the site.

The Congress for the New Urbanism had convinced HUD that a crucial element of planning was building new communities guided by development patterns common before the car was a major form of transport—which is why the HUD funding application for High Point had proposed a New Urbanist site plan. In fact, most communities in Seattle were built before World War II and therefore already had many of the key elements found in a New Urbanist community.

As a supporter of New Urbanism, I am most proud of how we successfully meshed a natural drainage system with the elements of a New Urbanist streetscape in the High Point redevelopment. The High Point streets, sidewalks, planting strips, and houses with front porches all follow the prescribed New Urbanist development pattern, and rainfall on the site is managed in an environmentally conscious way. The street pattern that evolved at High Point not only fit the site well but also made for a comfortable walking neighborhood. Providing an easy, safe walking environment is an important green element. Lanham Street, which is part of the north-south connection, was set so that it is parallel to the hillside on the eastern edge of the site. A review of aerial photographs from the 1940s shows that this location corresponds to what was once a dirt path. It was the route people took to traverse the site most easily. And today the location of this street still feels right. It fits the topography of the site.

Another choice we made was to keep High Point Drive a road on the perimeter of the site. One advantage of this was that we were able to keep many of the mature trees that lined the old High Point Drive.

Two other decisions also helped improve the site's walkability: Most of the time we separated cars from homes by building short east-west-aligned alleys for parking lots with room for fewer than twenty cars each. The smaller parking lots made it easier for neighbors to become familiar with which cars belonged in a lot and which did not. Residents needed to park their cars and walk past the front porches of other houses to get to their home. This was a way to encourage informal connections between neighbors. We also created several no-parking zones in the block where fire trucks could set up in case of a fire, and we put fire hydrants closer to the middle of the block to create additional locations for fire trucks to park.

The locations of the streets and alleys were set by 2007 when this rendering of the site was completed. Other changes were subsequently made. The grocery store with a large parking lot was not built in the mixed-use site and the for-sale housing was built as townhouses or single-family homes, except in the mixed-use site. The elementary school changed its name to West Seattle Elementary.

The shorter east-west alleys also gave us an opportunity to place carriage units at the entry to most alleys. Our thinking was that it would be helpful to give residents in the carriage units the opportunity to act as extra eyes on the alleys and the parking lots. We eliminated the more standard, long, out-of-sight alleys as well.

The list of ways we reduced the impact of cars on the site was extensive. On the collector streets (slightly wider streets within the street network), we added traffic circles and extended the curb into the street to protect the roots of trees. The tight turning radius of the street required cars to slow down around corners. Some High Point residents complained to me after they moved into the new High Point that larger vehicles had trouble maneuvering in the neighborhood because of the tight corners and parked cars on the 25-foot-wide streets. My response to these complaints was to point out the safety benefits, in a community brimming with children, of forcing cars to slow down.

Sylvan/Morgan

Sylvan/Morgan, the curving arterial (a street to deliver traffic from collector streets or other arterial streets) that runs through High Point, is important to how the neighborhood functions. For the past sixty years, the width and design of this arterial allowed cars to go faster (40-plus mph) than the speed limit (posted at 25 mph), creating a safety hazard for pedestrians and unpleasant street noise. Sylvan/Morgan did not even have a planting strip to buffer pedestrians from the speeding cars. Because the street felt unsafe, crossing it was an unnerving experience. The result was that High Point was effectively divided into two parts, with the popular major public park and the school on the side away from most of the residential homes.

Redesigning Sylvan/Morgan fit our larger goal of stitching High Point back into the fabric of West Seattle. A well-designed two-lane boulevard would force cars to slow down. Eliminating the barrier that speeding traffic created would make the street safer to walk along and to cross. The drive and walk along Sylvan/Morgan would be a welcoming experience, and the reduced traffic noise would make it more pleasant to live in a home facing the street. An added plus was that a narrower road would retain the space for housing that we needed to meet our goal of building 1,600 homes.

Although the City was not paying for the construction of the improved arterial—SHA was financing it and directing its construction—the redesign still needed the City's stamp of approval. Our first meeting with the City's road engineers in mid-2002 did not go well; in fact, it was terrible. The engineers, citing a provisionally modified road manual, said that Sylvan/Morgan had to have four traffic lanes, not the two we wanted, and that they could not justify a stoplight on the major walking route to the elementary school. The disagreement boiled down to a difference in philosophy about the purpose of roads. The traffic engineers believed that the primary, and possibly sole, purpose of roads was to move cars along as quickly and as efficiently as possible, while we had a broader view. We did not want an inefficient road, but we were unwilling to maximize vehicular efficiency at the cost of safety and livability for residents of the new High Point.

Our perspective about the function of streets eventually won out. Pedestrian-friendly streets, safe routes to school, traffic calming, and complete streets policies[63] were just beginning to gain attention. And today the decision-makers in the traffic division of Seattle's department of transportation share our philosophy.

Our specific successes included determining the road width, the right-of-way (ROW) width, and the number of lanes. We started with a fifty-four-foot ROW—the width of City-owned property measured from the outside of the sidewalks. The City's engineers originally required eighty-plus feet, although the road manual stipulated a ROW of seventy-six feet, a number we could have lived with. In the end, what helped us win the extra four-plus feet was learning that only the city council could amend the road manual, and that they had, in fact, not done so.

A seventy-six-foot ROW would still have accommodated four lanes, but we wanted a street that slowed traffic to a speed appropriate for children and seniors crossing. A boulevard would make it feel residential and allow us to narrow the effective width.

---

[63] The City of Seattle approved a Complete Streets Policy in 2007, which states that the Seattle Department of Transportation "will plan for, design and construct all new City transportation improvement projects to provide appropriate accommodation for pedestrians, bicyclists, transit riders, and persons of all abilities, while promoting safe operation for all users." Seattle Department of Transportation, Ordinance 122386, April 30, 2007, http://clerk.ci.seattle.wa.us/search/results?d=CBOR&s1=115861.cbn.&Sect6=HITOFF&l=20&p=1&u=/%7Epublic/cbor2.htm&r=1&f=G.

The compromise we settled on was a road with two lanes (each twelve-and-a-half-feet wide) with parking on both sides. The main intersection includes turning lanes. The new design provided embedded clues to drivers that they had to drive slower, in part because of the lane width but also because the road curved.

In the end, the newly built Sylvan/Morgan was probably our biggest victory for a walkable new community. Gaining approval for this turned out to be a marathon that took four years—during which time there was both a major change in the City's philosophy about building roads and a personnel shake-up throughout the City's department of transportation.

Today, Sylvan/Morgan is a two-lane boulevard with sidewalks buffered from the road by wide rain gardens and planting strips. It runs through rows of housing, all facing the street, and because of the relatively narrow lanes and cars parked along the street—part of our victorious design—traffic speed is considerably slower. There is also a traffic light at Lanham and Sylvan that benefits everyone, especially the elementary schoolchildren and their parents who walk to school.

Saving Trees

In 2002, before the bulldozers arrived, and while most of the original residents were still living at High Point, a group of ten- to thirteen-year-olds from the Youth Tutoring Program began discussing how much the upcoming redevelopment would disrupt their lives. Not only would they have to move but many of their friends would also be moving to different parts of the neighborhood or away from High Point altogether. Several of these kids were sitting in a tree while talking about this, and it suddenly occurred to them that that tree might actually be cut down. They knew the redevelopment called for stripping the High Point site of everything—the YMCA gym, the Head Start schoolhouse, rental units, sewers, roads, and electrical lines—and they assumed that the large trees would also be leveled.

This group resolved to work on saving all the big trees at High Point. Two members sent me a letter, which included the following:

> We've grown up in the High Point area and have come to know these trees. For us the trees are important because they provide a place to play, they make our neighborhood safer, they provide shade in the summer and shelter in the many rainy Washington months. Also they provide habitats for a large variety of animals, and animals need shelter just as much as people do. Have you ever seen a flock of birds emerge from a group of trees?

This group later gave a presentation to the council in which they demanded that all the large trees be saved. As a way to reinforce their demand, they gave names to their favorite trees.

That there was strong support for saving trees gave SHA the impetus to undertake a tree preservation program on steroids. We hired an arborist to do an analysis of the trees for vigor, structure, and preservation value. Then our architect and engineering (A&E) teams adjusted the location of the roads, parks, and houses to maximize the number of trees to be saved. They submitted a master plan application with a drawing showing which trees would be saved and which would be cut down. The sheet also showed where 3,000 new trees would be planted.

As construction began, we surrounded the designated trees with high chain-link fences that extended to the edge of the branches. We made a sign for each of the trees that included a warning that anyone caught damaging them was subject to a fine worth the value of the tree, including its replacement value. The value of the trees averaged out to about $17,000; a Great Sequoia on the site was valued the highest, at $71,596.

In 2004, this aggressive tree-saving project came back to bite us. As part of our planned replacement of low-income housing units, we donated a building site to a nonprofit housing developer for an 86-unit, subsidized, low-income building for seniors. Our civil engineering firm assisted the group in securing the necessary permits to build a new three-story building. The building plan called for a vehicle drop-off area at the rear entrance, because the front of the building did not allow for easy vehicle access. The problem was that, very close to the drop-off area, there was a tree marked to be saved on our site plan drawings, and the base of that tree was considerably higher than the back door of the building. Because the drop-off area needed to be level with the building entrance, the logical and only solution was to cut down this tree and regrade (lower) the site.

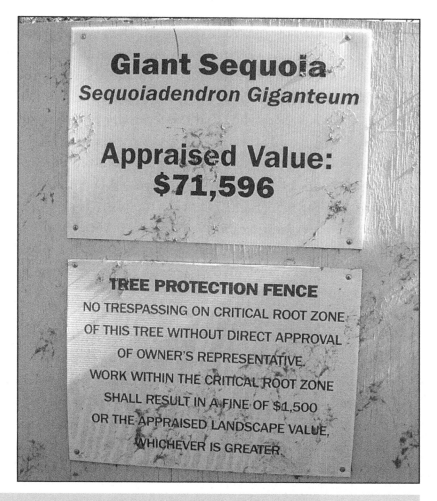

These tree signs were placed on the fence along the drip line of every tree.

To resolve this impasse, we turned to the City's building department director, Diane Sugimura. In Diane's office, high up on the twenty-fourth floor of the City office building, with its magnificent view looking south and east at Mount Rainier and Lake Washington, our design team and the City plans examiners were at loggerheads. Both parties made their case. The site plan called for the tree to be saved. The plan's checker, who worked for Diane, was intent on implementing the plan we had submitted; that was his job. We made a case for the tree to be removed because of the grading problem. We also argued, somewhat sheepishly, that the term *saved* on the construction drawing really meant *save in almost all circumstances*, but not this one. The large site drawing that showed our tree plan was open on Diane's conference room table, and something on the drawing caught Diane's attention. "It says here that they are also planning on planting new 3,000 trees," she said. Common sense won out, and the building was approved, with a replacement tree planted in a newly graded area near to where the old tree had stood.

After this standoff, we created a mechanism with Diane's department that allowed us to remove a saved tree if some crucial reason called for it to be taken down. This process required that we obtain approval for the species of replacement tree and that the trunk caliper of the replacement tree meet a certain reasonable standard. Some of the trees that we had to cut down have been preserved as part of the gate and small shed at the market garden.

Thanks to the members of the Youth Tutoring Program who got us started, our tree-saving plan worked well. A few evergreen trees fell over during a major storm that came through the site, and more recently, a few large deciduous trees that survived construction died from a tree disease. But otherwise, all but a few of the original mature High Point trees we saved during construction stand today and continue to play an important role in the community.[64] Their deep roots support the natural drainage system by helping to absorb rainwater into the ground, and their presence on the site is the one historic link between the old and the new High Point.

Remembering Thaddeus Soth

On August 28, 2005, 15-year-old Thaddeus Soth, one of the teenagers in the Youth Tutoring Program who played a vital role in saving the mature High Point trees was killed in a shooting that happened while he was sleeping over at a friend's house.[65] Thaddeus's loss was part of the passing of the old High Point era. No High Point teenagers have been killed since his death in 2005. The trees at High Point honor the memory of Thaddeus and other youths like him who have appreciated the power and beauty of nature in community spaces.

---

[64] In contrast to the overall success of our tree-saving plan, at least five major trees on the High Point Library site, built by the City of Seattle, which were not carefully protected during construction by the City's contractor, have died.

[65] *Seattle Times* Staff, "3 teens charged in fatal shooting," *The Seattle Times,* September 1, 2005, https://www.seattletimes.com/seattle-news/3-teens-charged-in-fatal-shooting.

Insights

Have a vision and stick with it. SHA and the civil engineers we worked with felt strongly about limiting Sylvan/Morgan to two lanes. We knew that four lanes with faster traffic would divide a community that was desperately trying to find its place among the City neighborhoods. It would also make it unsafe for children to walk to school and unpleasant for families to live in one of the homes fronting the street. Limiting this road to two lanes was an important professional stance for us and this new community to adopt.

Getting the street pattern and the street size right happened because we had a clear vision *and* were open to new ideas. We were adamant about the streetscape dimension, and we were open to designing a street grid that reflected the geography of the site. The design team gave me two alternatives for the street pattern early in the design process. One plan looked like streets in Seaside, Florida—the pattern originally devised by John Nolen, a planner New Urbanists like. The other plan was the one we eventually built. In making our decision, we chose to listen to the land. We came up with a pattern that fit the site and was our own application of New Urbanist concepts—a decision I am pleased we made.

CHAPTER 8

BREATHE-EASY HOMES

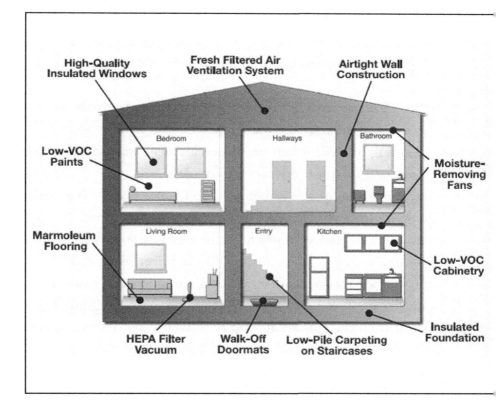

High-Quality Insulated Windows

Fresh Filtered Air Ventilation System

Airtight Wall Construction

Low-VOC Paints

Bedroom

Hallways

Bathroom

Moisture-Removing Fans

Marmoleum Flooring

Living Room

Entry

Kitchen

Low-VOC Cabinetry

HEPA Filter Vacuum

Walk-Off Doormats

Low-Pile Carpeting on Staircases

Insulated Foundation

This graphic highlights the special additional features added to the already healthy homes to improve the health of children with asthma.

What, No Photovoltaics?

In 2008, I gave a presentation on High Point's green features at an affordable housing conference in Chicago. Shortly after my talk, an attendee from Texas approached me and asked why there were so *few* green features at High Point. In his low-income development, each home had its own solar panels for generating electricity and heating water, and his team had built geothermal wells for heating and cooling. From my presentation, it was clear to him that we had no plans for these types of big-ticket green features at High Point.

This challenge to High Point's green credentials caught me off guard, and my response was flustered. I said that we had started planning in 2001 when green development was not the standard, and the more advanced technology was too expensive to implement on a scale as big as High Point's. But if I had gathered my thoughts better, I would have given a more nuanced answer. Our choices of green features at High Point were indeed constrained by cost, so crossing off the pricey items had been a no-brainer. Yet even with our budget restrictions, we made many smaller improvements that added up. We were designing High Point from the ground up, and there were decisions to be made at every turn. Once we embraced going green, the key to our success was making sure we considered green in every decision.

Being green is relative, based on geography, climate, and demography. I once visited a housing community in Taos, New Mexico, that emphasized both low energy use and low construction costs. The houses were built out of tires filled with concrete, and most of each house was underground, which made for stable indoor temperatures despite the desert heat. All the windows were on the south-facing side of the house, which consisted almost entirely of windows, a design that maximized the heat from the sun in winter. An extended overhang prevented the sun from overheating the house in the summer. Obviously this design would not have been appropriate for a redevelopment in West Seattle.

Some of the opportunities for green improvements at High Point were obvious from the start. For example, when choosing fixtures and appliances, subsidies from Seattle utility companies neutralized the extra cost of fluorescent light fixtures, ENERGY STAR° dryers, and front-loading ENERGY STAR° washing machines, which save both water and electricity. In other cases, our eye to creating a health-promoting, green environment steered us in the direction of solutions we had not originally thought of. When choosing building materials, we figured out that low off-gas, recycled products could be used in the kitchen and bathroom floors at little additional cost. In planning the front and back yards, we chose native, drought-resistant plants, which needed less water and also happened to be cheap. When we chose paints and adhesives, we again found that air-quality-friendly low volatile organic compound (VOC) paints and adhesives would not cost us extra.

Insulation was key in our green efforts. A well-insulated home blocks moisture from coming into the house, preventing mold growth and improving air quality. Good insulation also keeps warm air out of the house in summer and cold air out in the winter, reducing the energy needed to heat the house. We installed airtight drywall and high-quality double-pane windows and made sure all the penetrations in the building envelope were carefully caulked.[66] An independently administered blower door test—which uses a fan to pull air out of the house—showed that the houses were tightly sealed, which helped us to earn ENERGY STAR® approval.

We emphasized a health-promoting environment and reduced energy bills by choosing a gas-fired, high-efficiency, closed-loop boiler for both on-demand hot water and radiant baseboard heaters. Additionally, the radiators that are part of this system are never too hot to touch, making them safe for environments with young children. (Unfortunately, we selected a closed-loop boiler system that ended up breaking down frequently.)

However, even when we identified an opportunity for a green improvement, money was often the limiting factor. We were operating under per-unit guidelines, which we had to follow closely. Since our architects also worked for private home builders, we generally went as far with upgrades as the home builders were willing to go. In the end, we estimated that we added about 3 percent to our budget in order to include green items in the homes.

---

[66] You *can* have too much of a good thing when it comes to insulation, however; if a house is too tightly sealed, airflow becomes poor and the air feels stagnant. To combat this, we installed filtered fresh-air intake ports in all living spaces.

Green goals also had to be balanced with design goals, and sometimes the design goals won out. For example, when it came to the ceiling height of the rental housing, we opted for quality design over a strict energy-saving solution, increasing the ceiling height from eight feet (the standard for low-income units) to eight feet and six inches. The higher ceiling meant there was more volume and space to heat, but the trade-off in the spaciousness of the units was worth it.

A major part of our design vision for High Point was for the low-income housing to blend in with the market-rate units so that a visitor would be unable to tell which homes housed low-income families and which housed middle-income families. We also wanted High Point homes to harmonize with the traditional, older look of houses that populated the surrounding neighborhood. Our designs were intended to destigmatize low-income housing and demonstrate physically that High Point as a whole was connected to the larger community. We also chose to have nearly all rental homes, in groups of roughly ten units, with their front porches and stairs clustered around a small lawn ranging roughly from 700 to 1400 square feet. We intended these pocket parks to be places where young children (2- to 5-year-olds) could play under their parents' watchful eyes. This method of increasing community interaction would have been lost had we tried to maximize solar gain by orienting all the homes to the south.

In some cases, our eye to green did pay off during the design process. The zoning allowed us to build three-story buildings.

But we decided to build mostly two-story buildings by widening our 310 three-bedroom units by several feet and putting three rather than two bedrooms on the second floor, eliminating the need for stairs to a third floor. This not only reduced the amount of lumber used to build the home, but it also proved to be more energy efficient as there was less house volume to heat. The utility bills in these two-story three-bedroom houses were significantly less when compared to three-story three-bedroom units in other new SHA developments.

The Boiler Problem

I place the blame for the problems with the heating boiler system at High Point squarely on the shoulders of our design team (which I led) and our overall approach. In the early days of planning the new community, we were on a tear. We wanted to show the world how to build a great new green community. Unfortunately, this attitude, which led to other groundbreaking achievements, resulted in our mistakenly selecting an extremely unreliable hot-water system for 562 units (all of the rental units, except for those in the Calugus apartment building). The boilers break down frequently.

A review of the number of boiler-related work orders makes plain the extent of the problem. When a boiler that produces hot water for showers and the radiators stops working, a resident generally phones the management office. This phone call generates a work order. The maintenance crew—in this case, the most experienced member of the crew, because of the complexity of the problem— responds to the work order by going to the home to fix the problem. A no heat/hot water work order usually involves repairing or replacing the electrical circuit that controls the small boiler in a townhome unit. From 2014 to 2016 there was an average of 186 work orders per year to fix boilers. The number jumped to 420 in 2016.[67]

The High Point maintenance crew spends an inordinate amount of time trying to stay on top of this never-ending problem at the expense of carrying out the already difficult task of maintaining a site with 600 residential units. It has led to strains between the community members and the management staff.

How did this happen? I have not been able to sort out how our team made such a big mistake. I have learned that once a problem like this surfaces, few people are willing to step forward to talk about it because of the possibility of some kind of lawsuit. The only documentation I have found is a letter sent by the SHA Construction Project Manager to our architect, identifying the problem and asking for extra spare parts.[68]

It appears that this boiler problem is something that SHA leadership was willing to live with for about ten years. In 2018, SHA took another look at this problem and found a local supplier of boiler parts and began to fix the failing boilers.

---

[67] Seattle Housing Authority.
[68] Andrew Doherty, SHA construction manager, communication to Mithun, June 15, 2007.

Breathe-Easy Homes

In 2008, a powerful thirty-minute documentary, *Place Matters*,[69] was produced, featuring Lanh Truong and her son, Stephen, then five, who were residents at High Point. The documentary shows Stephen playing on a slide in the old High Point while Lanh speaks about Stephen's asthma and how disruptive his illness has been in their lives, especially when she needs to take him to the emergency department for treatment. The scene then switches to the two of them playing catch on the lawn in front of their new High Point Breathe-Easy Home (BEH). Stephen is wearing a superhero costume, and his mother's voiceover attests to the reduced number of asthma attacks Stephen has experienced and the greater ease in her life as a result of his improved health.

The genesis for the High Point BEH program can be traced to resident leader Bonita Blake. Sometime early in the planning process, Ms. Blake raised the possibility of doing something about the indoor air quality of the new High Point homes. People were experiencing health problems in the mold-infested 1940s' units.

Tom Byers, the consultant we had hired to explore ways to make High Point green, was friends with Dr. James Krieger, a Seattle-based national expert on asthma in low-income families. As a result of their connection and the concerns expressed by Ms. Blake, we submitted a successful grant application to HUD to build thirty-five homes for children with asthma. The grant was awarded in

---

[69] Ellie Lee, *Place Matters* (California Newsreel, 2008), transcript at https://unnaturalcauses.org/assets/uploads/file/UC_Transcript_5.pdf.

concert with a research project to study the asthma-control benefits of a BEH. This research project introduced our team to the world of scientific studies.

The grant's principal investigator was Dr. Tim Takaro who, together with our design team, drove the process of deciding which features to add to the already green rental homes. According to Dr. Takaro, costs of emergency-department treatment for an asthmatic child are high: One hospitalization for an asthma attack costs between $4,309 and $8,044, or roughly the cost of a one-time per-unit upgrade, which came in at $5,123.[70] The big-ticket item was the whole-house HEPA (high-efficiency particulate air) filtration and fresh air ventilation system. Another requirement was carpeting on the stairs only, which made the interior of these homes somewhat sterile-looking as compared to the other units; the rest of the flooring was a non-off-gassing, green linoleum-like product called Marmoleum. The houses also had additional insulation below the concrete slab foundation that reduced the moisture level in the house as well as several small moisture-reducing fans built into the walls. We provided a special floor mat to wipe dirt off the bottom of shoes.

We made a conscious decision to spread the Breathe-Easy Homes around the High Point site, instead of bunching them all together. We did not want to stigmatize the people living in these units.

---

[70] "Hospital admissions were too rare to have a meaningful measure for our study, but we did measure the reduced number of urgent and emergency clinic visits. This went from $250/year to $80/year for the group of 34 children in the study. So a conservative estimate of this saving alone is $1,430/year per person over two years without considering medications, hospitalizations, lost work, etc. If we prevented just one hospitalization, that savings alone would be between $4,309 and 8,044." Tim Takaro, email message to author, July 25, 2019.

The idea of building homes especially for children with asthma hit a responsive chord with the public. Seattle and Vancouver, Canada, newspapers carried stories on the homes, and the project had wide coverage on the Internet. But even with this support, the biggest challenge for the BEH program was finding families to live in the homes. We needed to find thirty-five low-income families who had a child with asthma to live in a BEH and participate in the research. Given that the incidence of asthma runs at 10 percent in low-income populations, above the prevalence for the general population,[71] we thought it would be relatively easy to find these families. Yet Denise Sharify, the Neighborhood House project manager who was responsible for finding candidates, called the recruiting process a nightmare.[72] This was in contrast to the relatively easy rent-up of the non-BEH High Point units.

Some of the obstacles resulted from our interest (as required by the grant) in demonstrating scientifically that the program would have a significant impact on the health of the children and their families. The protocol required testing the children's health one year before moving into the BEH, again when moving in, and finally one year after. The families had to agree to sign a special lease that stipulated no smoking in the house and prohibited the family from having a furry pet. The grant also paid for a new vacuum cleaner as well as new pillows and mattress covers to reduce dust.

[71] Richard Perry, George Braileanu, Thomas Palmer, and Paul Stevens, "The Economic Burden of Pediatric Asthma in the United States: Literature Review of Current Evidence," *Pharmacoeconomics* 37, no. 2 (2019): 155–167.
[72] Denise Sharify, interview with author, May 27, 2017.

Some potential candidates did not believe that the BEH units would help their children. This may have stemmed, in part, from a general mistrust of SHA. Language and cultural barriers also played a role; in spite of the availability of interpreters, it was difficult to communicate just how a different house would improve a child's asthma symptoms.

But the proof was in the results of the study, which showed that there was no question that the health of children with asthma living in the Breathe-Easy Homes had improved. "Children and adolescents with asthma who moved into an asthma-friendly home experienced large decreases in asthma morbidity and trigger exposure."[73]

The question that is difficult to answer, even for researchers, is whether the children's asthma symptoms improved solely because of the extensive asthma-friendly upgrades we made in the homes or due to other reasons, such as moving into a new home or a new community. Other factors might also have accounted for, or contributed to, their improved health, but in a real-world setting like ours, it was not possible to control all of the circumstances. The primary study did show that as compared to the experience of families who received home asthma education visits only, "those who moved into a BEH experienced additional improvements in a wide range of outcomes and trigger exposures."[74] Figure 6 summarizes the results of the BEH study.

---

[73] Tim K. Takaro, James Krieger, Lin Song, Denise Sharify, and Nancy Beaudet, "The Breathe-Easy Home: The Impact of Asthma-Friendly Home Construction on Clinical Outcomes and Trigger Exposure," *American Journal of Public Health* 101, no. 1 (January 2011): 55.
[74] Takaro et al, "The Breathe-Easy Home," 58.

FIGURE 6. Benefits of moving into an asthma-friendly Breathe-Easy Home

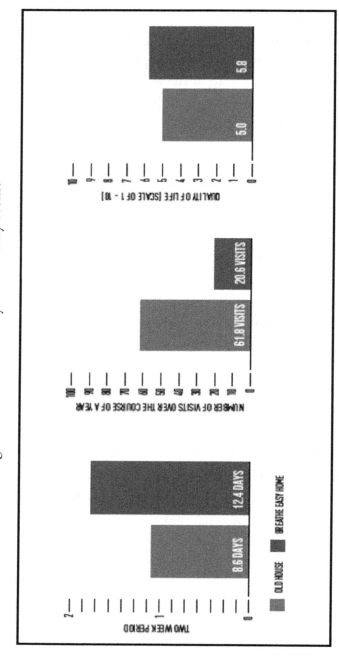

Illustration by Vincent Bachman, Line by Line Creative.

Once in the new home, the children's symptom-free days in a 14-day period dramatically increased from 8.6 days to 12.4 days. The number of urgent visits required to treat asthma attacks decreased by over 60 percent annually. These and other positive changes made a marked improvement in the quality of life for the children's caretakers (parents, in most cases). When caretakers were asked to rate their quality of life on a scale from 0 to 10, with 0 being the lowest, their quality of life improved from a rating of 5.0 to 5.8.[75]

What is most significant about the improvements depends on the point of view. From a public policy perspective, fewer trips to the emergency department can be measured financially. It is harder to place a quantitative value on other outcomes of the Breathe-Easy Homes, such as the opportunity for a child like Stephen to enjoy a more pleasant life and perform better in school due to fewer asthma attacks, while reduced stress levels for parents like Lanh have benefits that reach beyond home and family life.

Building Green Challenge: Breathe-Easy Homes

We were pleasantly surprised that all of the construction crew members were highly supportive of building the Breathe-Easy units and had no problem following the special rules established to build these units, such as not smoking in the units.

[75] Takaro et al, "The Breathe-Easy Home," 59.

The only problem we encountered was that the special air filtering system used in these homes had to be cleaned, and these systems were initially in the attic. In Phase I, these filters were difficult to reach from the attic opening. In Phase II, they were placed in a far-more-convenient-to-reach attic location.

"You're Taking Too Long in the Shower!"

This is a line from the play a group of High Point teenagers put on in fall 2005 to creatively channel their unhappiness with the newly redeveloped community. The teenagers had spent the previous day with a local improvisational coach hired by energetic community builder Kari-lynn Wenciker to help them work out their concerns about the new High Point.

Moving to a new rental home meant having to deal with new utility charges.[76] In the new High Point, neighbors were faced with bills for metered water usage in addition to bills for natural gas (for heating water as well as the house) and for electricity. Long showers were now an indulgence for which most parents were unwilling to pay.

Were tenants connecting with the conservation message, and were the new green features in the rental units making a difference

---

[76] Low-income residents pay 30% of their income for rent plus utilities, so they pay 30% of any increase in utility charges.

to overall resource use? Doris Koo, then president and CEO of Enterprise Community Partners, pushed us into finding out.

Doris knew our work and felt that there was an opportunity to compare the utility bills at High Point with the bills at NewHolly, the first major SHA redevelopment, which had been built in the late 1990s according to the Seattle Energy Code of the time. Residents at the two redevelopment sites shared similarities in ethnicity, income level, and family composition, and there were enough units at each site for a statistically reliable sample. Plus, NewHolly was located in Southeast Seattle, which had weather conditions comparable to High Point. Doris was willing to have Enterprise pay for the study because she was interested in demonstrating the payoff to going green.

The study, conducted in 2009, compared utility consumption and bills in the low-income housing units at High Point and NewHolly.[77] The substantial savings shown in the report supported our belief that the additional efforts we had taken to green High Point were worth it. According to the report:

> Residents at New Holly [*sic*] use about 6% more water than those at High Point, 11% more electricity for lighting, [and] 37% more natural gas for water and space heating. … [In terms of cost,] at 2007 rates for gas and electricity, residents of an average 1,175 square foot unit at High Point saved approximately $235 per year compared to a resident of the same size unit at New Holly.[78]

[77] In exchange for SHA generating the utility billing records needed to conduct this study, Enterprise Community Partners granted SHA $125,000 to build twenty-five additional Breathe-Easy units in Phase II, which would begin to be occupied in the summer of 2008.

[78] Enterprise Community Partners, *Sharing the Benefits of Building Green: A Study of the High Point Community*, 2009, p. 3, https://www.enterprisecommunity.org/download?fid=8411&nid=4617.

Additionally, the study found that requiring residents to pay utility bills—which was the case at both redevelopments—had the impact we had hoped for: "At New Holly [*sic*] and High Point, where housing units are individually metered for water use, about 70% of the residents report 'taking extra steps to save on water.'"[79]

The housing authority continues to calibrate its billing system for water usage so that SHA maintains some ability to reward conservation and discourage overuse. The system they currently use relies on national studies of utility use for energy-efficient homes and provides an incentive for families whose energy use is less than the average use. The energy bill is adjusted for family size and building size. Families are charged extra for use that is substantially above the average use.

One of the recommendations, from an interview with residents carried out as part of the study, was that the on-demand water heaters, which provided an endless amount of hot water, should be outfitted with timers. As far as I know, there was no follow-up to that recommendation, and parents are continuing the time-honored tradition of yelling at their kids to get out of the shower.

Insights

Establish your level of commitment to green early on. It was helpful that we started planning for building green homes early in our process. For example, the decision we took early on to

---

[79] Enterprise Community Partners, *Sharing the Benefits*, 4.

build two-story (rather than three-story) three-bedroom units was integral to the building layout plan. In this way, we did not miss opportunities such as giving the contractor time to organize building the walls off-site. Another consideration was determining the capacity and interest of our contractor to actually build what we wanted. Because the contractor's representative sat in our meetings, his firm was committed to our green goals and saw ways to use them to its benefit. For example, they saw efforts to seal the interior of the units as a way to monitor the work quality of their subcontractor.

Due diligence. With regards to the high failure rate of the boilers, it is clear that it is critical to carry out thorough due diligence in selecting essential components such as heaters and hot-water systems.

Listen to High Point neighbors. They have wisdom to pass on. Bonita Blake knew from her many years as a resident leader that many others in the community had respiratory problems, but we would not have known this if she had not told us. Indoor air quality is important and should be considered a priority green objective. Given our commitment to green, creating what we did was not that much harder.

PART 4
BUILDING THE
COMMUNITY

CHAPTER 9

CONSTRUCTION AT HIGH POINT

One of the valuable items "farmed" from the twenty old structures as part of deconstruction, shown stacked here, was structural decking. It could be old growth tongue and groove, given that it was used to build the old units in the early 1940s.

Deconstruction

Before construction could begin, we needed to remove all of the old public housing units from the site. Thanks to a fortuitous set of circumstances, we had a chance to test the feasibility of deconstructing, rather than demolishing, these 60-year-old structures. The Seattle Public Library, which purchased a site from SHA, had plans to build a new High Point branch library ahead of our schedule for clearing all of Phase I. We had to clear the library site early, so we had an opportunity to run a deconstruction on a smaller scale.

Deconstruction means "the careful dismantling of a building roughly in the reverse order that it was assembled such that components are reusable and have significant economic value."[80] We were eager to explore this method of clearing the site. It was a potential alternative to trucking the material to a landfill. We tested the idea by hiring an experienced deconstruction company from Portland to take apart a duplex. This experiment gave us hope that it might be economically feasible to deconstruct more of the old units.

Next we issued a solicitation for contractors to bid on the deconstruction of twenty units as part of the Phase I construction documents. We found a contractor who bid to do the work, but the price he offered ($5,323/unit) was higher than a standard demolition contract ($3,826/unit).[81] This was primarily because this contractor was not willing to lower his bid in anticipation of selling some of the material he had "farmed" from the old buildings. We

---

[80] Seattle Housing Authority PowerPoint presentation.
[81] Seattle Housing Authority spreadsheet, April 3, 2003.

had hoped there would be some economic value to the material in the homes, but that was not the case, as it turned out. Therefore, in spite of other benefits of deconstruction—such as its value as a training environment for workers new to construction, and less material going into the landfill—we reluctantly proceeded to demolish the old units in the conventional way. In addition to the extra costs, deconstruction was slower than standard demolition methods.

The deconstruction process made it clear how unhealthy living in the old units had become. Once the walls were opened up, we could see the extensive mold that had built up over the years.

Rain

SW Juneau St. is underwater following a record rainfall just as construction began and before all the rain collection measures were in place.

Nothing seemed out of the ordinary about the weather on October 20, 2003. It was raining, which happens frequently in the fall in Seattle. Phase I construction had begun earlier in the season. The Phase I housing, concrete streets, and all but the important trees we were saving were gone. The general contractor had begun to install the systems needed to hold water on-site to prevent dirty rainwater from making its way to Longfellow Creek.

Someone from the site called in the middle of the day and said it looked like there was a rainwater problem at the site. I headed out to the site to take a look. I remember thinking that there was an unusual amount of standing water on the highway as we drove the twenty minutes from our downtown office to West Seattle. Once we got to the site, about all we could do was look at the mess and take pictures.

The next day, we learned that more than five inches of rain had fallen the day before, shattering the city record for rainfall in a 24-hour period.[82] There was a plume of brown water visible at the mouth of Longfellow Creek, but there was no way to officially identify our site as the sole culprit for the turgid water.

High Point's size and uphill position meant the construction contractors had to up their game to limit the quantity of muddy rainwater flowing off the site and down to Longfellow Creek. The state had also placed more stringent standards on our Phase I general contractor; for example, the contractor had to place

[82] Daryl C. McClary, "Washington State Has Its Driest Summer on Record in 2003," HistoryLink.org, December 29, 2003, https://www.historylink.org/File/5630.

special water-retaining fences around each block and make sure that vehicles leaving the site had mud washed off the wheels. After the big rainstorm, the contractor established a variety of techniques to manage the rainwater, including building temporary ponds around the site. The idea was to direct rainwater that fell on-site to the ponds. The pond water was then pumped through filters and run through pipes that left the site.

Fast-forward to the spring of 2004. I can still remember exactly where I was when I got a frantic call from Thomas Nielsen, our person in the field overseeing construction. "Tom, the ground is undulating! What should I do?" Thomas was dismayed to see large dirt-hauling trucks *bounce* as they drove over a recently filled temporary construction pond area right in the middle of the High Point site. We would be building housing at this location soon, and the bouncing was a warning sign that the process of filling the pond with dirt had somehow left the area unsuitable for building. No wonder Thomas was agitated.

However, although my responsibilities as the senior development manager included overseeing construction alongside numerous other planning and coordination functions, calling me to get construction advice was like calling me for fashion tips. I knew almost nothing about the actual management of a large construction contract. My experience was limited to remodeling a kitchen and bathroom in my own home.

We were a lean operation. My core team consisted of Thomas Nielsen, one other more junior construction expert, and me.

Of course, there were other colleagues in the development department I could call on as well as various consultants on our A&E teams. Once the panic caused by the bouncing truck subsided, we concluded, with the help of a soils engineer on our A&E team, that the soil the contractor had used was too wet to achieve proper compaction. It was replaced with drier soil.

Overall, the contractor, Absher Construction, was proud of the job they did and the lengths to which they went to keep dirty water from leaving the site. On the other hand, when we were faced with needing to bring in drier soil, some of the design team felt that parts of the plan's execution were not as strong as they could have been. Differences of opinion were common during construction.

There were multiple eyes on the construction to prevent things from going terribly wrong. SHA had two construction experts, the architects had another, and our numerous engineers were always on the site checking progress, as were several inspectors from the City. I was never comfortable with the sense that there was an underlying lack of trust between the owner (SHA) and the contractor. The general fear came from the concern that the contractors would want more money than they were entitled to. It is not that people did not talk to each other. There were weekly construction meetings with owner and contractor representatives. But on a job the size of High Point, there were many unknowns and opportunities for distrust.

Another factor that led to friction between the two sides had to do with expectations. Our team had enjoyed great cooperation and enthusiasm during the design process and had high expectations for what could be built. For the contractors, this was another construction job they had won that would be good for the company's bottom line. The differences in expectations led to some inevitable conflicts. Ironically, in 2016, when I interviewed Doug Orth, the main contractor's senior project manager, he said that he is most proud of the High Point work, which was over and above everything else he has done in his long construction career.

This machine breaks up the concrete from the old roads, leaving smaller pieces to be broken up and used as part of the new roadbed.

Construction Comes to a Halt

We faced another near disaster roughly halfway through the infrastructure construction of Phase I. Each of the two phases of construction had an infrastructure contractor (responsible for grading, sewers, and roads) and a housing contractor. In Phase I, the housing contractor was the *prime*, meaning it was in charge of the entire site. Generally, the housing contractor starts to build the housing units once the infrastructure is in place.

Less than halfway through building the infrastructure in Phase I, the infrastructure contractor took all of its equipment off the site permanently and sued the housing contractor for whom it had been working. It did not take long for the housing contractor to turn around and sue the housing authority. All construction came to a halt. People were reluctant to share information because of the lawsuits, so we did not know exactly what was going on. We were told that the dispute had to do with the lack of a written contract between the infrastructure and housing contractors, but we doubted that that was the real story.

After about two months, many depositions, and two mediation sessions, work started back up with a different contractor. Merlino Construction stepped up and offered to finish the infrastructure work within the allocated budget.

Ten years later, I was told that the dispute had been over money. The infrastructure contractor believed that it had underbid the job and that walking off the site was the least costly alternative. Part of the reason it underbid had to do with something called pipe jacking. This is a construction technique used to tunnel under objects such as large trees. In the case of High Point, the plans called for using pipe jacking in order to run electrical lines under trees on the "dry" side of the street. With High Point's unique street design, one side of the road right of way was the wet side where water was directed into a swale. That left the other side of the road as the only path for the electrical lines, which we had decided to put underground. Evidently, the on-site supervisor for the infrastructure firm that walked had mistakenly believed that his pipe jacking estimates were too low and that carrying out the pipe jacking would result in his firm losing money on the job. Merlino Construction had no trouble pipe jacking under trees.

Commons Park

We had always planned for the redeveloped High Point site to include a large park (3.5 acres) meant to serve the entire community. It was dubbed *Commons Park* early on and was to be built as part of Phase I. Working with our parks consultant, we came up with a relatively flat park design with an open field, concrete paths, low curved seating walls, a water feature, and play equipment for children. We had designated $1 million to build the park in the middle of the site, but the contractors' bids came in at $1.8 million. As a result, we put off building the park until Phase II, roughly two years later.

As we got closer to Phase II, the conversation at our weekly planning sessions turned to the question of how do we build a great park within our budget. We brought in Melinko Matanovic from the Pomegranate Center to brainstorm design ideas and turned the park design over to our civil engineering firm (SvR), which was also a landscape design firm.

During Phase I construction, we had let the general contractor store excess dirt—what is referred to as a contractor's laydown—in the shape of a mound in the middle of the future Commons Park. Too much or too little dirt is a big deal on a large construction project. Because we still had that mound of dirt on the site, we came up with the idea of building a high point at High Point. We would transform that existing mound into part of the new park, saving some money in the process by not having to dispose of the excess dirt.

We agreed with SvR to simplify the design, and they took over preparing the bid documents. According to Matt Suhadolnik, SvR's park designer, they made the design appear simpler by reducing the number of drawings detailing the specifics to be built from about twenty drawings to eight. They did this, in part, by halving the scale of the drawings such that one inch on the map equaled twenty feet (rather than ten feet) on the ground. They made some other changes, such as creating an accessible path on the mound and eliminating some concrete paths in the park.

The changes resulted in a bid of $800,000, a price we could live with, and the park was finally built.

A school which used the Neighborhood House facility during the year holds its graduation at the amphitheater.

Community Amphitheater

Ever since hearing a talk by my friend Paul Fishberg, I was looking for a way to add some type of spiritual element to the High Point community. Paul had taken a leave of absence from his job as executive director of the Delridge Neighborhood Association (the Delridge neighborhood is adjacent to High Point) and traveled around the world studying communities. He reported back that every community he visited had some type of spiritual feature. I thought we should try to add this at High Point. During our discussion about the scaled-back park design, we decided to build an amphitheater into the south-facing side of the mound. The amphitheater had the potential to be that spiritual element.

Melinko was in charge of designing and overseeing the construction of the amphitheater. He understood that by creating a gathering space in the shape of a circle, he would be replicating a powerful feature used in ancient Greek and Roman communities to bring people together. He used large boulders to create a semicircle seating pattern to anchor the seating in the circle. The large boulders added to the sense of place—to the spiritual feeling of the space, some would say. He created a backdrop to the circle that featured panels with wood carvings of birds from six of the continents—an idea that was generated in our meeting with a group of High Point students. To top it off, Melinko had a large phoenix drawn in the middle of the circle to represent the community rising anew.

When we designed the porch and stairs on the north side of the Neighborhood Center, we made sure the space blended seamlessly into the amphitheater. If you have the chance to visit High Point, have a seat on one of the boulders in the amphitheater and see if it does not feel like it has been there a very long time.

"Boulders from Heaven"

The contractors left these boulders at the edge of the site, so we turned them into features in this playground. Here neighbors gather for a block party.

We used the area off the eastern edge of the site up against the cemetery fence to store material during construction. It was an out-of-the-way place where for-sale housing would be built in Phase II. After all of the affordable housing was built and the roads were in place, the contractors took their trailers and equipment off the site. However, they left us a present. We called it "boulders from heaven."

Much to our surprise, the contractors had been surreptitiously moving very large boulders they encountered during construction to this out-of-the-way area. But when we asked, the contractors said they did not know where the boulders had come from, thus they became "boulders from heaven." It would have been expensive to take the boulders off-site to a fill area, so we had the contactors push them to areas near saved trees.

Successful Affirmative Action Program

Our development team met frequently with Frank Bosl and John Hallgrimson, two brokers we used to find the for-sale home builders. These men were among the most successful commercial brokers in the Seattle region. John would marvel frequently about how complex our job was as compared to the work his private clients managed. Meeting affirmative action goals was important to the housing authority and one of the tasks we took on that John's private clients did not.

Part of our job was to make sure that the contractors we hired worked aggressively to meet WMBE (Women- and Minority-Owned Business Enterprise) goals when procuring goods or services.[83] Our WMBE track record for both phases of construc-

---

[83] "Women and Minority-Owned Businesses," City of Seattle, accessed July 27, 2019, http://www.seattle.gov/city-purchasing-and-contracting/social-equity/wmbe.

tion was solid, thanks in large part to Absher Construction, which also had a strong commitment to the WMBE program.

Our affirmative action efforts had three components. First, of the business subcontractors hired by Absher, 40 percent of Phase I and 33 percent of Phase II subcontractors qualified under the WMBE program. The second facet involved hiring High Point residents or other low-income neighbors who would qualify. Absher hired fifty-five Section 3[84] (low-income residents from the neighborhood) residents in Phase I and seventy-four residents in Phase II. The third effort undertaken by Absher was working with unions to bring in apprenticeship workers in order to get them on a path to well-paid union jobs. In Phase I, 38 percent of the union workers were in the apprenticeship program; in Phase II, the apprenticeship goal of 29 percent was achieved.

Creative Bidding Process

By early 2006 we were ready to request that bidders submit proposals to build Phase II. I was happy to discover that government has the ability to do something other than selecting the lowest bidder to do the job. Other approaches have been developed as a result of (and to avoid) the shortcomings of the lowest bidder concept—that is, where the least experienced or least qualified bidder can more easily submit a low bid.

---

[84] "Section 3 Requirements for Owners, General Contractors, and Subcontractors," City of Seattle, accessed July 27, 2019, https://www.seattle.gov/Documents/Departments/Housing/HousingDevelopers/ProjectFunding/Sec3_05a.doc.

The housing authority has the ability to take advantage of an alternative bidding process called the *General Contractor/Construction Manager Procedure* (GC/CM). We used this alternative method with the infrastructure bidding on Phase II of High Point, and it was a win-win for SHA and the selected contractor.

The GC/CM process allowed us to consider the proposed cost as only one factor among several in selecting the contractor. We asked bidders to tell us how they would approach such issues as team experience with erosion control and sustainable projects, plans for hiring from women- and minority-owned businesses and Section 3 workers, and creative job cost savings shared between the owner and the contractor. It was Tri-State Construction's response to the creative job cost savings category that got it the contractor job.

To understand how these cost savings worked, I need to explain that we first leveled the playing field in the bid documents with our assumptions—a common practice. We told the contractors to assume that all excavated native material (dirt) would be removed; then, when dirt was needed later as fill, imported "good" soil was to be used. This was to ensure the quality and durability of all of the places where dirt would be used as part of the new construction. Tri-State, in their proposal, committed to a plan that shared the savings that could be realized on the job by using selective good soil found in the process of their work on-site. This would save money, because this good soil would not have to be disposed of, and other good soil would not have to be purchased. This creative approach would save

SHA about $1.3 million and meant that the $33.044 million project came in at the budgeted amount. The losing bidder submitted a challenge to HUD, which had the final say, but the creative bidding process withstood this challenge, and Tri-State Construction was fully signed off on as our Phase II contractor.

Getting Help Overseeing Construction

It was only toward the end of the six-year construction process that I finally figured out a way to feel comfortable in my role overseeing construction. Things had changed in the development department, and my new boss, SHA's development director, Stephanie Van Dyke, had considerable construction experience.

We were in the final stages of building the 600 affordable units, and we were frustrated because it felt like the contractor was not staying on top of the project. The solution Stephanie and I came up with was arranging for her to meet the contractor's top person on the site once a week. With this weekly check-in, we could be sure there was a chance to focus the contractor's attention on what his crew was doing, and I felt reassured that the project would turn out as planned, because Stephanie had looked it over.

Insights

Deconstruction is a powerful green technique worth trying under the right conditions, such as when the building to be deconstructed has materials that can be sold readily, when a slower schedule can be accommodated, and when you want to create training opportunities for workers.

Selecting a contractor. We used a GC/CM approach for bidding and the infrastructure contract for the work. This type of contract tends to decrease the animosities that I found cropped up more easily with a more traditional lowest-bidder construction contract. Alternative approaches are worth considering, and other methods for selecting a contractor can work, too. For example, on my last project, we used the RFP (Request for Proposals) process, which worked well. Here is how a competitive RFP works, as described by Stephanie:

> At the schematic design stage we select a contractor who works with us and the A&E firms to assist in developing the schedule, budget, community participation plan; and to be involved in the design process. The goal is to have a set of documents that all parties are committed to that reflect the best approach to the project. We select the GC [general contractor] based on qualifications and on price for predevelopment services, price for general conditions work during construction, and profit. At the 50 percent construction drawings stage, there is a check to make sure the design

implements the decisions the team made, and then the GC bids out the components to subcontractors.[85]

Management skills vis-à-vis construction experience. The late George Rolfe, a former professor in the Runstad Department of Real Estate at the University of Washington, gave me some good advice about how to approach being in charge of a major construction project while having little construction experience. He said the answer was not to try to become an expert in elements of construction but rather to use management skills to achieve the desired goal. Some of the main skills I used on this project were to (1) study the problems and understand what was going on, and (2) get at the basis of disputes by talking to people on both sides, using communication skills to resolve the differences. Being a manager, to me, means, in part, hiring good employees, the right employees, and giving them a great deal of authority.

---

[85] Stephanie Van Dyke, email message to author, June 25, 2019.

CHAPTER 10

HOME BUILDERS
AS PARTNERS

For-sale builders took full advantage of the land we sold them overlooking the pond. These are single-family homes.

"Tom, you need to get over here right away! There's a bunch of kids out of control running around on the lawn in front of my house. If I could sell my home, I'd move right now!" My heart sank when Tony Welch said this to me over the phone early one afternoon in April 2006. I had been counting on Tony, his wife Sarah, and other homeowners like them—people who got it, who understood what we were trying to create at High Point—to help make the neighborhood work. Tony and Sarah were among the homeowners who, I thought, had bought into High Point not only for its good real estate value but also because it promised to be a good neighborhood with a wide variety of residents. Was the behavior of a group of unruly boys going to turn homeowners against renters and in turn bring home sales to a standstill?

It turns out that events similar to this one with the children would be an ongoing area of tension in the community and, in fact, are an issue in mixed-income neighborhoods countrywide. National studies of mixed-income communities indicate that "unsupervised children and youth at and around the development seem to be an issue of particular contention." [86]

The Welches were some of the first middle-income homebuyers. When I got Tony's frantic call, he and Sarah had been living at High Point for only a few months; their low-income neighbors had moved in more than a year earlier. This was one of the first nice days of the year, and the new neighbors had not yet had a chance to get to know one another.

---

[86] "The Nature of Social Interaction in Mixed-Income Developments," Mixed-Income Development Study, Research Brief 3, The University of Chicago School of Social Service Administration and Case Western Reserve University Mandel School of Applied Social Sciences (November 2009): 7.

I told Tony I could not make it out to High Point right away but that I would make some phone calls. Two hours later, around 5:00 p.m., I drove the twenty minutes from my office to the small park in front of the Welches' home. The property manager and the head of the private security force[87] both showed up at the same time I did. But there were no kids playing in the park. Tony emerged from his front door wearing a T-shirt that revealed bulging biceps and several tattoos. "Hi, Tom. We figured it out," he said. "My wife and I made some lemonade and gave it to the kids. We talked to them about some rules they would have to follow if they were going to play out here—like no swearing—and they said fine."

I felt a great sense of relief. This was the best possible resolution. The Welches had understood that the kids were just looking for a place to run around on a nice day. And maybe the kids—who probably thought of Tony, a union electrician, and Sarah as "rich"—had been testing their new neighbors. In the end, the adults had acted like adults, and the kids had showed that they would respond positively when approached with friendship, clear expectations, and respect.

The Game Plan

Tony's phone call had caused me concern for good reason. High Point's financial viability depended on families like the

---

[87] High Point management has employed a private security service since High Point opened. This service is for evening hours.

Welches choosing to buy a home there. More specifically, it depended on 500 middle-income families buying homes there. We were counting on families purchasing homes at prices comparable to other long-established middle-income communities in West Seattle.

Our plan called for SHA to build all the infrastructure: roads, sewers, parks, sidewalks—all of it. We would build low-income housing on some blocks and set aside other blocks for middle-income housing. We would run the bidding process to allow experienced homebuilders to submit proposals for the designated for-sale blocks; we would select the builders and review their plans against a set of design guidelines that supported our vision for the site, such as New Urbanist and green principles. It would then be up to the builders to design, build, price, and sell the homes. Finally, SHA and the builders would run a joint High Point cooperative marketing campaign to promote the community.

Adding value was an ever-present part of my thinking about High Point. As far as I was concerned, every decision, no matter how small, had to be filtered through the question of whether it would detract from or add value to the site. My goal was to have the homes sell for as much as possible—with the exception of the units set aside for affordable home ownership, which we subsidized. This is why I pushed for things like undergrounding the electrical lines and putting in something other than the standard, ugly, cobra-head streetlights.

As High Point was SHA's third major mixed-income redevelopment, we had experience with selling land to homebuilders. In fact, I spent my first three months at SHA changing the for-sale housing business model in the housing authority's mixed-income communities. Prior to this, SHA's construction contractor had built the for-sale homes with the assistance of an experienced developer. SHA had also set the sales prices and made all the decisions about which features to include in the homes. The revised business model meant that it was my responsibility to find reputable builders and have *them* build the homes; that way, *they* would assume the risk of building and selling homes. We took SHA out of the home-buying process and focused on finding good builders and selling them blocks with infrastructure in place for them to build on.

At SHA's first two sites, we generally separated the rental homes from the for-sale homes by putting the for-sale blocks on the edge of the sites and the low-income rentals in the middle. Even though these were mixed-income communities, we avoided mixing low-income housing and middle-income housing on the same block. The thinking was that such a mix might lower the value of the for-sale homes. When it came to determining the location of the for-sale sites, another rule we usually followed was to place for-sale houses across the street from other for-sale homes, rather than have a row of for-sale homes face a row of rental homes. Builders had made clear that this was the setup they preferred.

Our original plan for High Point had been to follow this model from the two other sites, even though the geography of High Point meant that doing so would afford views of Puget Sound and the Cascade Mountains to only the for-sale homes; the rental homes would be in the interior of the site with no views. Since we were trying to maximize the return from the sale of the for-sale blocks, this pattern made sense from a purely economic perspective.

In early 2003, our architectural team came up with plan A, which followed these original guidelines. Everyone involved up to that point was pleased that the same pattern could be applied to High Point and that the site could accommodate the proposed 1,600 housing units. But, as mentioned earlier, when we took plan A to one of our Partnership for High Point's Future meetings, we encountered serious pushback. West Seattle neighbors, business leaders, and the low-income renters at the meeting all objected strongly to saving the best views exclusively for the middle-income for-sale buyers. It was clear to me that I would not win with the argument that we needed to follow this model in order to maximize our economic return.

Plan B, which we showed the group a few months later, and which we eventually followed, had a good number of the view lots set aside for rental housing. There were still more view lots for the for-sale homes, but we had now created some balance, as shown in Figure 7. The views are on the eastern edge of the site.

FIGURE 7. Final layout of the new High Point site, showing Phase I and Phase II. Views of Puget Sound and the Cascade Mountains are to the east of the site.

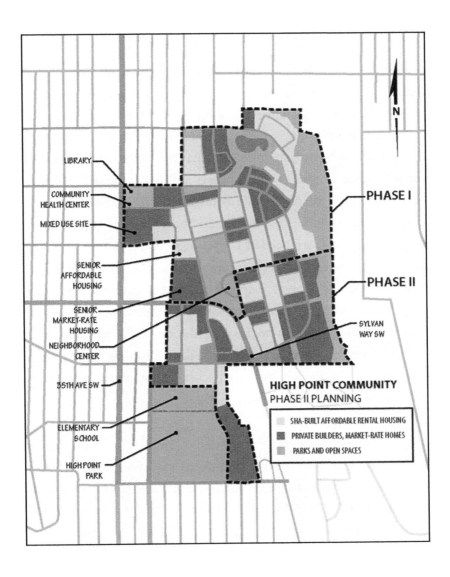

Phase I for Sale

In March 2004 we were ready to test the waters to see the level of interest from homebuilders.

A month earlier, we had hired Suzanne Britsch of Real Vision Research Inc. to study the possible absorption rate by building types (attached or detached townhomes, stand-alone homes, etc.) in "the package." There were to be roughly 275 homes for sale in Phase I. In order to maximize our financial return, we needed to consider these homes as one package, and this package needed to be a variety pack offering a wide assortment of house types at a wide range of price points. This meant that homes had to be of different sizes and styles; there needed to be single-family homes, carriage units, townhomes, and condominium flats. The idea, which Real Vision advised us on, was to appeal to the largest number of buyers by providing as many choices as possible. Suzanne's report laid out how many single-family homes, townhomes, flats, etc., we could expect to sell per month and suggested the appropriate price points. We included this information in a packet that our team of commercial real estate brokers distributed among potential builders.

Luckily for us, Real Vision estimated the home price sales at far below what buyers were willing to pay. For example, they estimated the high end of the range for a three-story townhome at $340,000. In fact, homes sold for $455,000—or $115,000 over the estimate. The price of the single-family detached homes ended up being $180,000 more than the original estimate.

We figured that the builders knew better than we did about how to take advantage of each site. So the builders selected the lots they wanted and recommended the types of houses they would build, along with the arrangement of the houses on the block. They also told us how they expected to price the homes, based on the Real Vision study and their knowledge of the market.

It was our job to set up the sale offering in such a way that builders did not compete head-to-head for the same product (houses) at the same price point. Figure 8 shows the variety of product and price points that we settled on.

FIGURE 8. Estimated selling prices for Phase I homes for sale at High Point (2006).

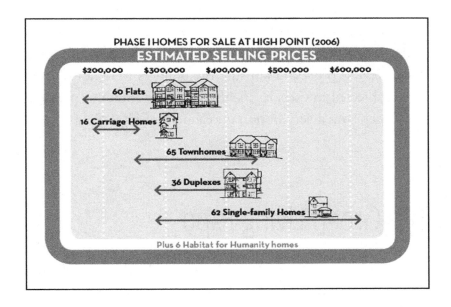

We were worried that the builders might propose some homes that would not be in sync with our thinking for the site and thus make the site less attractive and of lesser value. Therefore we created a High Point design book that was the basis for our design review process of the builders' drawings. The book stated, "The design guidelines call for drawing upon the best of the architectural traditions found within Seattle neighborhoods. These include simple building forms, fall roof pitches and roof overhangs, uncluttered roof lines, usable and protective front porches and stoops, formal acknowledgment of the street from the home, vertical window proportions and variety of color. The houses will be built as a community, not a hodgepodge of contradictory developments sharing a street."

The City's building department reviewed all of the builders' proposals according to the City's health and safety standards. In addition, builders were required to submit their designs to both the design review process carried out by SHA and the City design review process. I am sure the builders were not pleased to be subjected to extra layers of review, but from our perspective, design was a very important element of High Point.

The Green Living Expo

SHA ran a competitive RFP process to identify a marketing firm that could partner with selected builders and the housing authority to "develop and manage a cooperative marketing, advertising promotional, training public relations program to generate optimal home-buying traffic and maximize value of the community of new homes for sale." In summer 2005, the housing authority selected the successful vendor: Fusion Partners, a Seattle-based firm specializing in marketing and communication programs for master-planned communities.

Fusion Partners came up with a bold plan that served multiple purposes. It proposed a grand opening exhibition for selling houses at High Point in Phase I—what became the Green Living Expo. At this stage, most of the rental housing in this phase had been built, which meant that if the for-sale builders hustled, they could have product for the public to view. This was a good way to create some buzz within the Seattle home-buying market and present High Point in an entirely new light. By this time, we had already set High Point on its green path by building the natural drainage system and the Breathe-Easy Homes. The expo gave us an indirect opportunity to encourage friendly competition between the builders in their green efforts.

We had established a minimum of green performance for the builders. We required that they participate in the Master Builders Built Green Program at the three-star level. To encourage the builders, we provided them with a consulting team of experts on green building who gave technical assistance with green products and also showed ways to display the green products in the homes.

Three of the builders added green features beyond the Built Green program's requirements, in part because they liked the idea and in part because their homes would show better at the expo. The other two builders saw the green requirements as the price of doing business with us. One builder, Fred Armstrong from Devland Homes, recalls that he and his partner got caught up in some of the green frenzy and ended up spending more than they should have on some of their homes. "We put in the most energy-efficient heat pump available, and we found oak floors that were recycled from the Cleveland High School gym, and we used bricks from the kiln in Oregon."[88]

Another builder plumbed in units to accommodate a solar water heater. He installed solar panels in one of the units as a demo, but was unable to convince any buyer to pay the additional costs to have the solar panels installed. We concluded that buyers were cost-conscious and unprepared to pay an additional $5,000 to lower hot water bills.

The ambitious Green Living Expo worked. For two weekends in September 2006, High Point teemed with prospective homebuyers, West Seattle neighbors, and many others curious about this new green neighborhood. The weather was good, and the site was decked out with custom-designed banners proclaiming the new High Point and explaining the green features. To make this happen, Fusion Partners created an extensive partnering program that included, among other things, substantial marketing opportunities and product demonstrations, such as a van outfitted with solar

[88] Fred Armstrong, personal communication with author, September 2006.

panels. Visitors to the expo could view exhibits in a large tent and tour the builders' new model homes as well as completed but not yet occupied ENERGY STAR®-certified affordable rental homes.

A few of us, bullhorns in hand, took large groups of people on walking tours of the site. Many volunteers served as docents in the for-sale model units, where green features were labeled carefully. People seemed to have a great time. The sidewalks were full of visitors kicking the tires on this new green neighborhood.

I am not sure where the estimate of 7,000 visitors for the two weekends came from, but that certainly seems to be a reasonable number. At the end of the two long weekends, the housing authority communications manager approached me with a big grin. She had just overheard a low-income resident comment, "You can't believe how great it is to finally live in a neighborhood that other people actually want to visit."

FIGURE 9. Sample promotional material from the Green Living Expo at High Point (2006).

Our cooperative marketing efforts continued for the next year and a half. We met periodically with the builders to review both how we were spending our marketing money and how we could keep our message fresh. We placed ads in suburban newspapers and Seattle papers like the *Seattle Gay News*. We also placed higher-cost ads in the *Seattle Times'* "New Home" Saturday insert. We sent out email blasts to consumers and real estate agents. We updated the High Point web page frequently. And—my favorite tactic—we placed bootleg signs all around West Seattle. These were A-boards promoting open houses held by High Point builders. We referred to them as bootleg signs because we did not have the necessary permit for them.

Revenue to SHA from the For-Sale Home Program

In the months following the expo, we started to receive positive sales reports from the builders. Over the next two years, the number of sales and the prices far exceeded our expectations. Our total land sales for 251 units was $18.3 million. The highest-priced home sold for $575,000. Our profit participation totaled nearly $3 million. When we sold each block to a builder, we negotiated an "established" sale price for each home. This was the estimated sale price that we felt would constitute a fair price given the land value. Our agreement called for us to split 50-50 any net sale proceeds over the established price. Our thinking about this profit participation program was that sale prices over the established price were a reflection of market forces that neither the builders nor we had much control over. If the home sale market happened to increase, then it was only fair that we should share in this additional revenue with the builder.

Selling 251 homes was powerful evidence that we had significantly changed the perception of High Point from a dangerous neighborhood to something quite positive. Within a few years, the financial burden of living next door to a project had been lifted, and private landowners began to take advantage of the increased value in their land as well as the improved perceptions of High Point.

Two other indicators of this change of perception in the neighborhood were significant, because they came about directly as a result of the dramatic effect the redevelopment had on the neighborhood. First, new houses were built on five empty lots directly adjacent to or across a street from High Point. Along the western side of the community, fifteen new homes were constructed on deep lots, each with the capacity to hold more than one home. Previously these lots had had only one house. A second indicator of the change in perception about the High Point community came as a total surprise. High Point's neighbor to the northeast is the Forest Lawn Funeral Home and Cemetery. A few years after home sales had begun, the cemetery director told me that their business had doubled since the redevelopment. He speculated that families now felt comfortable about having their relatives buried adjacent to the new community.

CHAPTER 11

RECESSION

A section of Phase II, as it was eventually built out, with both rental and for-sale housing. The green area (top right) is the Forest Lawn Cemetery.

The Grocery Store That Never Was

Since the late 1990s, it had been clear that having a grocery store at High Point was important. The successful HOPE VI application called for a grocery store to be located on 35th Avenue SW, the arterial on High Point's western edge. The whole Delridge neighborhood, which High Point is a part of, is a food desert. A grocery store was a high priority for the neighbors and the housing authority, not only because it was desperately needed but also because it could provide a common meeting ground for High Point residents and other neighbors.

On August 22, 2002, a representative from the Albertsons grocery store chain delivered to SHA a Letter of Intent stating that Albertsons wanted to build a grocery store at High Point. SHA signed the document but did not make an announcement about Albertsons's interest, because we knew doing so would be premature.

At one of our first meetings with Albertsons's representatives, we made it clear that we required any store to be in a mixed-use building, with the store on the ground floor and apartments above it. We gave examples of other mixed-use projects in Seattle, including Uwajimaya in the International District. Albertsons contacted Lorig Associates, Uwajimaya's developer, and later decided to use Lorig to build the store and the housing above it. We then started negotiating with Lorig's team as well as with Albertsons.

It was at one of the early meetings that I committed a major blunder. While Albertsons agreed to have housing on top of their store, they insisted that there had to be a large parking lot *in front* so that potential shoppers could see that there was plenty of parking available. This rule of thumb in the grocery business is in direct conflict with the principles of New Urbanism, which call for buildings to be built right up to the sidewalk with parking either underneath or behind the building.

I was the sole representative of High Point at this particular meeting. As a strong advocate of New Urbanism, I argued that this was an unacceptable parking solution for the store. Instead of compromising by suggesting I confer with my colleagues at SHA, I stated that the Albertsons grocery store could not be built at High Point. That was the last discussion with Albertsons, and regrettably, it was the last time a grocery store expressed interest in building at High Point.

I have often thought about what might have happened if I had been less insistent about the location of the parking lot. I do know that if the proposal had come in several years later, the Seattle land-use zoning code, which was revised in 2006, would not have permitted a parking lot in front of the building. In addition, Albertsons went through some restructuring in 2004 and 2006, which might have affected the deal as well. But even so, I think that my stance at the meeting was not in High Point's best interest and that the benefits of a grocery store outweighed the issue of terrible land use. Unfortunately, there is no do-over for my decision.

I spent another eight years at the housing authority trying to secure a grocery store, or at least some commercial activity, at High Point. As it turned out, the window for building a grocery store was open for only a short time. Common real estate guidelines that tend to rule out building grocery stores in low-income areas came into play. Also, West Seattle is a peninsula, which means its population could support only a limited number of grocery stores. As it was, over the next several years, three new stores were either announced or built within two miles of High Point.

Despite the limited odds of getting a grocery store after Albertsons withdrew, we kept trying. For example, we solicited the services of Security Properties, a developer who had experience working with mixed-use buildings. We went so far as to lower the company's taxes for seven years through New Markets Tax Credits, but this was not a big enough incentive for Security Properties to overcome the obstacles to signing up a grocery store. We then worked with Lowe Enterprises on a plan to build a mixed-use building on 35th. Those negotiations went on for over a year, but Lowe, like other developers, backed off from its interest when the recession hit.

Not securing a grocery store for High Point is one of the biggest pieces missing from the original High Point vision. Although it is difficult to assess its impact on High Point home values, not having a store definitely made buying groceries a larger burden on low-income families.

Phase II for Sale

In November 2006, we put land for 250 to 300 for-sale home lots on the market for homebuilders to bid on. Again, the exact number of homes that would be built depended on the site lays proposed by builders. By this time, we had built all the roads and sewers and were completing the construction of the last of the 600 low-income units; nearly all of the Phase I for-sale homes had been sold. We contacted our brokers and asked them to prepare a package to market the land. The brokers presented us with the builders' offers, and all seemed to be going well. We selected five builders, all relatively small companies that built fewer than fifty homes a year. One of our stalwart builders, Polygon NW, had not bid on the property, but since we had enough other offers, that did not worry us. In retrospect, it should have.

Jailbirds

Much to my surprise, working on High Point brought me face to face with two men who are famous in Seattle for serving time in federal prison. The more notorious of the two was Frederick Darren Berg, "the man who bilked investors out of more than $100 million in Washington's biggest Ponzi scheme."[89] Mr. Berg's criminality was not then known, and his homebuilding firm successfully bid to build homes in Phase II on one of our prime sites. We worked primarily with Mr. Berg's associate, but he did attend at least one meeting. His firm wanted to build about thirty green homes. They withdrew their offer, along with the other successful bidders, when the housing market collapsed in 2008. Mr. Berg was sentenced in 2012 and escaped from prison in 2017 while serving an 18-year-term.

We spent much more time meeting with the other former federal inmate, Charles "Chip" Marshall III. Chip worked for a California development firm that proposed building an apartment with a grocery store on our mixed-use site. That deal also fell victim to

[89] Mike Carter, "Frederick Darren Berg, mastermind of Washington state's biggest Ponzi scheme, escapes from California prison," *The Seattle Times,* December 7, 2017, https://www.seattletimes.com/seattle-news/crime/frederick-darren-berg-mastermind-of-washington-states-biggest-ponzi-scheme-escapes-from-california-prison/.

the housing recession. Chip was one of the Seattle Seven, a group of Vietnam War protesters who pleaded no contest to contempt of court charges in 1972 and spent three months in prison.[90]

In late 2007, the builders began dropping out slowly. By mid-2008, we had no builders and no prospect of paying off a $28 million line of credit with Bank of America. We had spent the $28 million primarily on building the infrastructure for Phase II.

The Seattle Housing Authority was now in financial crisis.

SHA's annual operating budget at the time was about $66 million, so we owed nearly half our annual budget and had very little in reserve. Our approach to redeveloping High Point had a built-in financial risk, because we built all the site infrastructure for the for-sale builders long before we received payment for the land. The builders paid us back several years after they had built and sold houses on the site. While there had been housing recessions in my lifetime, we had not anticipated the Great Recession. I recently located a spreadsheet I prepared in March 2008 that showed an assumption that revenue from builders would be forthcoming as planned. Many of us involved in selling homes could not get ourselves to believe that there would be a housing bust.

Reading reports about the housing authority in Kitsap County on the other side of Puget Sound did not make us feel any better about our prospects. The housing authority there had built a con-

---

[90] Kit Bakke, "A crash course in court proceedings," Protest on Trial, *The Seattle Times,* May 6, 2018.

dominium that had undersold, and the lender was now insisting on immediate repayment. The Kitsap Housing Authority, however, had received a guarantee from the Bremerton City Council that it would pay off the loan. We had no such guarantee.

I flashed back to 2001 when I first considered taking the High Point job and half-joked with my future boss, Al Levine, that I was hesitant because I was afraid I might bankrupt the agency. What had been an abstract concept felt like a real possibility in late 2008.

The Cavalry to the Rescue

"I'm uncomfortable with being called a hero or saying that we saved the day. We were just building homes. That's what we do."[91] This was Gary Young's response when I told him that we thought of his company, Polygon NW, as the cavalry coming to pull the housing authority out of a serious financial hole in late 2008.

We—along with all the Phase II builders we selected—had been oblivious, or chosen not to pay attention, to the dangers inherent in the frenzy of the home-buying market leading up to mid-2007. Gary and his partners, however, had been uncomfortable with what they saw in the housing market, scaled back their business, and built up their reserves to weather the coming storm. They continued to build elsewhere in the region, but at a slower pace, and

---

[91] Gary Young, personal communication with author, February 27, 2017.

kept an eye out for the right opportunities. In late 2007, High Point's offering did not look like a good business opportunity.

That Polygon, a longtime Northwest homebuilder, would ride in and save the day is easier to understand with several years of hindsight. SHA had worked with Polygon on and off since 2002. It had been the first outside builder to purchase lots at our original HOPE VI redevelopment, NewHolly. Polygon had also been the biggest builder in Phase I of High Point, building a condominium and a number of single-family houses and townhomes.

Polygon had been patient. It knew that there would continue to be some demand from homebuyers for new homes at the right price, and it wanted to keep operating. It also knew, or at least anticipated, that interest rates would stay low so that buyers could afford to purchase their first home more easily.

By early 2009, the housing authority was prepared to deal in terms of giving Polygon a discount on the value of the land that was ready to be built on. This was a difficult decision for us to make, because we knew that what we had already created at High Point had a great deal of value. But we also knew that no other reputable builder was interested in our land. Our standard profit participation clause made the decision a little easier.

The prospect of having a for-sale builder sign up to buy land at High Point and to build new homes provided SHA with a potential source to pay off the just over $28.5 million line of credit we owed the Bank of America. It was necessary to show the bank's loan officers that the High Point property would be sold. The challenge involved convincing the bank that the most likely way to be paid back would be to allow SHA to continue to be responsible for selling the land to builders—in other words, that the bank should not try to sell the land itself or turn it over to some third-party seller.

The housing authority struck a deal with the bank that required SHA to turn over the land sales proceeds from both High Point and our other ongoing redevelopment, Rainier Vista. SHA was given four years to make quarterly payments to pay off the loan. In addition, we had to pay interest equaling $3.47 million on the loan and repay any funds from the sale of land no later than fifteen days following the receipt of the revenue.

On November 16, 2009, the housing authority board of commissioners, its governing body, passed a resolution that formalized the payback process to the bank. Finalizing this deal marked the end of an era for SHA's development department. The oversight I had operated under for many years was being tightened, and budget considerations would play a bigger role in nearly every decision.

SHA made the last payment to Bank of America on January 31, 2013, and we were finally out from under this debt. Over 35 percent of the funds to pay back the bank came from the sale of 171 Polygon townhomes and single-family houses. Another large share of the funds came from the sale of land at Rainier Vista. The housing authority also sold the two buildings housing their staff; today, SHA leases their office space. As of spring 2020, the remaining Phase II for-sale lots had been sold to builders, and the last roughly thirty new homes were being built.

Impact of the Housing Recession

The first High Point for-sale homes first came on the market in 2005. The sales and the prices came out of the gate very fast in 2006 and 2007 with 25 and 28 sales respectively. However, sales came to a near standstill in 2008 (12 sales), 2009 (3 sales), and 2010 (4 sales). Sale prices also took a big hit from the recession. It took nine years for the median price of townhomes to exceed its pre-recession high ($419,990); in 2017 the median price reached $544,990. There is an important caveat to the home sale prices from 2018/2019. The prices are high partly because builders were selling the larger homes on lots with premium views. Now that these homes have sold, the median price will probably be closer to West Seattle prices.

One conclusion to draw from the sale record at High Point is: If you're going to build a mixed-income development, do it in a strong home sale market. High Point had the wind at its back and was able to weather, albeit with wracked nerves, the severe national housing market collapse.

Home Sale Prices at High Point

Home sale prices at High Point have held up well as compared to the rest of Seattle and to West Seattle. Yes, the great views of Puget Sound, the Seattle skyline and the Cascades help to increase home sales values, and the pond, tree canopy, and master-planned community also add value. However, there are other factors at play in the community[92] that have the potential to dampen the home sales prices. These include the residual impact of the red line drawn in the 1930s that put High Point on the "wrong side of the tracks" (in this case the east side of 35th Avenue SW) and, as a result of community input, the for-sale blocks are more mixed in with the affordable housing vis-à-vis SHA's other HOPE VI sites.

Table 4 shows that High Point home prices track with the healthy. In fact, they were part of the Seattle market, which had the fastest-rising home prices in the country for two years (2016–2018).[93] The table includes the sale price of both new homes and the resales of homes sold within the boundary of the master-planned community.[94]

A review of fourteen years of High Point home sale prices shows that High Point along with the rest of Seattle successfully weathered the drop in home prices triggered by the great housing recession. The median price in Seattle in 2018 was $790,000, compared with the median price at High Point of $617,500 and in West Seattle $665,000. In 2019, High Point homes went up to $702,500 while in all of Seattle prices stalled.[95]

---

[92] See, for example, the beginning of Chapter 10, a homeowner threatening to move.

[93] "Unlikely Record: Region's Home Prices Didn't Budge for a Year," *The Seattle Times,* June 26, 2019.

[94] The High Point subdivision is named on the legal title of all lots within the community.

[95] Rami Grunbaum, "Seattle is 'a notable exception' for stalled home prices," *The Seattle Times,* June 25, 2019, https://www.seattletimes.com/business/real-estate/seattle-is-a-notable-exception-for-stalled-home-prices/.

The median sale price of High Point single-family homes increased at a steady pace since 2010, reaching $702,500 in 2019. The price increases mirrors the increases in all of West Seattle. (Tables created by Heartland LLC.)

TABLE 4. Information assembled by Heartland LLC

Median Sales Value 2005-2019 *(2019 through May)*

Data Source: King County Assessor

Single Family Homes	2005	2006	2007	2008	2009	2010	2011	2012	2013	2014	2015	2016	2017	2018	2019
Seattle City Limits	$395,000	$444,000	$490,000	$455,000	$414,200	$415,000	$394,000	$412,000	$450,000	$490,000	$553,000	$627,000	$720,000	$790,000	$775,000
West Seattle* except High Point	$348,000	$386,450	$417,000	$399,950	$360,000	$358,000	$331,500	$341,000	$370,863	$408,000	$476,500	$507,435	$600,000	$665,000	$665,000
High Point	$0	$423,812	$492,495	$493,500	$380,000	$280,000	$308,813	$315,000	$365,080	$416,180	$479,400	$525,000	$640,929	$617,500	$702,500

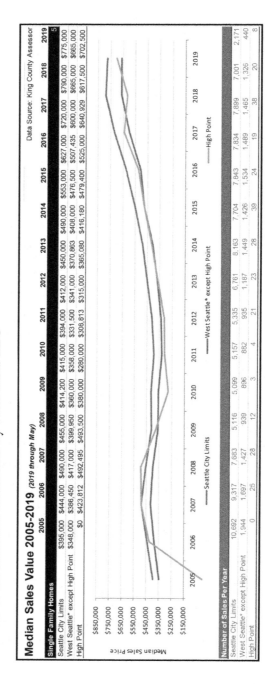

Number of Sales Per Year	2005	2006	2007	2008	2009	2010	2011	2012	2013	2014	2015	2016	2017	2018	2019
Seattle City Limits	10,692	9,317	7,683	5,116	5,099	5,157	5,335	6,761	8,163	7,704	7,843	7,834	7,899	7,001	2,171
West Seattle* except High Point	1,944	1,697	1,427	939	896	882	935	1,187	1,449	1,426	1,534	1,489	1,465	1,326	440
High Point	0	25	28	12	3	4	21	23	28	39	24	19	38	20	8

High Point townhome prices increased steadily from 2012. As of 2019 they roughly matched the $560,000 price recorded in all of West Seattle.

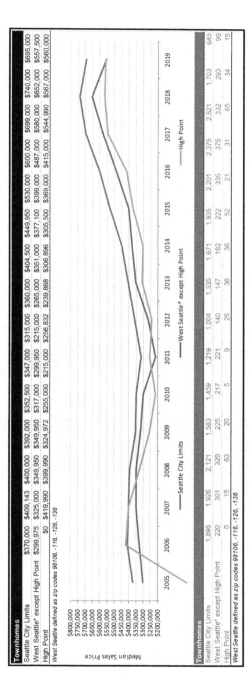

Townhomes	2005	2006	2007	2008	2009	2010	2011	2012	2013	2014	2015	2016	2017	2018	2019
Seattle City Limits	$370,000	$409,143	$400,000	$392,000	$352,500	$347,000	$315,000	$360,000	$404,500	$449,950	$530,000	$600,000	$699,000	$740,000	$695,000
West Seattle* except High Point	$299,975	$325,000	$349,950	$349,950	$317,000	$299,950	$215,000	$265,000	$351,000	$377,100	$399,000	$487,000	$580,000	$652,000	$557,500
High Point	$0	$419,990	$399,990	$324,972	$255,000	$215,000	$256,832	$239,868	$306,896	$305,500	$369,000	$415,000	$544,990	$567,000	$560,000

West Seattle defined as zip codes 98106, -116, -126, -136

Townhomes	2005	2006	2007	2008	2009	2010	2011	2012	2013	2014	2015	2016	2017	2018	2019
Seattle City Limits	1,898	1,926	2,121	1,583	1,459	1,219	1,004	1,335	1,671	1,935	2,201	2,375	2,521	1,703	645
West Seattle* except High Point	220	301	329	225	217	221	140	147	182	222	335	375	332	293	99
High Point	0	15	63	20	5	9	25	36	36	52	21	31	65	34	15

West Seattle defined as zip codes 98106, -116, -126, -136

Is High Point Being Gentrified?

A February 15, 2014, front-page story in the *Seattle Times* quoted a Federal Reserve Bank study that concluded Seattle was second only to Boston in the degree to which gentrification had spread throughout the city since 2000. This article included a map of nine Seattle census tracts that showed signs of significant gentrification since 2000 based on increases in home values, income, and percentage of college graduates. High Point was on this map.

A coffee shop opened on the ground floor of a market-rate apartment building on the mixed-use site in late 2019. The building has underground parking. This is the site where we were unable to locate a grocery store after we couldn't work out a deal for it in 2002. (See Page 179.)

While gentrification is occurring on some blocks at High Point, the big picture is that there are 675 housing units—42 percent of the community—that have been set aside for low-income residents. These 675 units will always house low-income residents. The incomes in the home values of the other 925 units will increase in the future, but because of the public ownership restrictions on the 675 units, the neighborhood will not experience the across-the-board transformation associated with gentrification.

Insights

Find ways to stay at the negotiating table. When it came to losing the grocery store, there may have been a solution to putting the parking lot in front of the store. I should not have shut down the meeting because we could not agree to an approach right then. It was too big a decision. I should have at least said, *Let's meet again next week and see if there is a solution that works for both parties.*

Managing financial risk. Was there a way to avoid the terrible financial hole we put ourselves in? With a conventional master-planned community, it is possible to have for-sale builders build and pay for the infrastructure needed for their homes. If we had used that approach, our debt would have been much smaller. However, some of the redevelopment's unique circumstances made that approach nearly impossible. Creating the natural drainage system did not allow us to separate out sections of the site; it is a holistic system that needed to be built at one time. (The only thing we deferred was putting down the final layer of asphalt on the street in certain sections of the site.) The patchwork pattern of rental and for-sale units across the site also required us to complete the entire drainage system in one go.

Changing stigma is possible. One High Point achievement that should not be overlooked is that we changed the stigma associated with housing east of 35th Avenue SW. This was a team effort, and it came about through many stages, as a by-product of our marketing as well as the attitude of younger homebuyers who had knowledge of the history of 35th Avenue SW as a dividing line in the community and perhaps also wanted to be part of a positive change.

PART 5
LIVING AT
HIGH POINT

CHAPTER 12

MULTIFACETED MANAGEMENT

Neighborhood House, a LEED gold building, provides meeting rooms for the community, office space for service providers, and Head Start classrooms.

Multiple Organizations Run the Community

Zach Chupa, High Point grounds supervisor, told me recently that it has taken him many years to figure out which of the multiple plants do well at which location at High Point. The same can be said about High Point residents in general. They are a complex mix of people from extremely varied backgrounds who have come together in a new environment. Most have grown to be comfortable in this new environment. Some were never comfortable and have since moved out.

Long before any construction began, our team put in place three entities to operate in the new community: the Open Space Association (OSA), the Homeowners Association (HOA), and the Neighborhood Association. SHA, as the developer of this master-planned community, was entitled to establish these associations.

SHA has played a varied role in each of these associations. The housing authority continues to have three members on the OSA board. With HOA, once enough homes were purchased (by 2015) the homeowners took control of this board. A homeowners association is a private nonprofit association created by the developer—in this case, SHA—primarily to govern all of the private homes in the community. Families living at High Point ran the Neighborhood Association and its current iteration, as was always intended. In order to obtain part of the financing for

High Point, SHA also established two other entities to manage the rental housing: High Point North and High Point South.

The Open Space Association

When we started to plan for managing the community, we realized that High Point's unique green features called for launching an association that would have the resources and authority to make the 120-acre site look really good. Our goal was to meet landscaping standards usually found in well-established, middle-income communities.

We called the new organization the Open Space Association (OSA) and gave it responsibility for all the parks, planting strips, sidewalks, and trees. In effect, we were placing High Point's fate in OSA's hands. If OSA could not manage the green spaces well, it would jeopardize the community's real estate value. Although we understood from the beginning that the landscaping was important, we had no way of knowing that it would become the community's most cherished feature. It was, and still is, in OSA meetings where community leaders have had to step up to insist on a high standard of maintenance and to resolve issues that arise from the site's unique landscaping complexity.

In order to operate OSA, we brought together the key institutions on the site and gave them a place at the table. Here they could exercise their mutual self-interest and creatively fulfill their responsibilities for "providing site-based maintenance of these facilities (storm-water swales, common open space areas, mature trees, parks and major pond feature) using the most progressive green and low-impact methods and tools, and organic landscape maintenance techniques available."[96] The OSA board, kept small to facilitate decision-making, consisted of three homeowners (appointed by the HOA), the High Point property manager (the person who oversees the rental housing), and two SHA representatives.

SHA also gave OSA authority to collect fees for site maintenance. Every year the board determines the amount of money each housing unit will pay monthly to maintain the site. Each homeowner pays the same per-unit amount that the SHA management team pays for each of the 600 rental units. By 2017, the monthly OSA bill was $63.[97]

If I were to describe High Point's appearance in one word, it would be *verdant*—green and lush with plants, grasses, and vegetation—and this is its best feature. Everyone who lives there loves this about the site, but the flip side is the challenge of maintenance. Adding to this challenge initially was the tacit understanding—which I naively promoted, because it sounded so good—that this greenery would be maintained without resorting to the use of herbicides and pesticides. After all, the system of channeling rainwater was called a *natural* drainage system; it did not seem natural to use chemicals to rid the site of weeds.

For the first roughly ten years, the unofficial policy of not using artificial chemicals to kill weeds was effective. For example, on the short street Julie and I lived on, residents would wake up to the smell of clover, which had been spread on the weeds between the cement blocks that made up the road bed. Site-wide, the landscaping crew would manually uproot the weeds.

The OSA ran smoothly until 2013, when a number of disparate events occurred that pitted homeowners against one another in a public dispute. Zach Chupa, who had been supervising the OSA grounds crew, left for graduate school. Zach is a charming, driven man, and he was committed to High Point's green values. His mission was motivating his landscape crew to make High Point shine, and he did exactly this for many years through hard work, landscaping knowledge, and encouraging his crew to buy into his vision.

Zach's departure occurred just as the new Phase II Polygon homes were being sold and new homeowners were moving in. Evidently, Polygon did not play up the green commitments on the site, such as the natural drainage system, when selling the homes. More to the point, the new homeowners were not told of the expectation that the landscaping needed to be main-tained without the use of herbicides and pesticides in order to keep chemicals from going into the pond and eventually into Longfellow Creek and Puget Sound.

Enter Deborah Vandermar, a relatively new homeowner at the time who had moved to the site specifically because of its green features. Like Zach, Deborah was dedicated to the High Point landscaping ideals of no herbicides or pesticides. She had the time and the leadership skills to mount a community-wide effort to fend off the use of chemicals to kill weeds and called her effort *Keep High Point Green.*

With Zach no longer on-site, conditions deteriorated. A group of new homeowners demanded that the verdant site be spruced up, advocating the use of chemicals to get rid of the weeds that had grown unchecked. Deborah went into high gear and organized an extensive community-wide weeding effort. Working with the OSA, SHA, and SPU, she obtained a $22,000 Neighborhood Matching grant. She organized homeowners and renters into teams to weed the site. She even recruited an old High Point friend, Gary Thomsen, to make videos in four languages showing people how to weed. Over the course of this successful effort, 400 different individuals gave 1,000 hours of service to the cause. Slowly, the site began to look better, but the consensus was that volunteer weed pickers were not a long-term solution.

Through fortunate happenstance, Zach came back in December 2014 to once again run the landscaping crew. The team got the site in good shape, and Zach is now working on a plan that will keep High Point's landscaping looking good even if he, at some time in the future, is no longer leading the crew. Such an effort may even require the judicious use of herbicides, which were never, it turns out, formally prohibited from the site, in spite of comments by others and me. As of June 2019, OSA was running well under Zach's leadership.

The Homeowners Association and the Carballos

Around 9:00 p.m. one Sunday evening, just as Julie and I were winding down from the weekend, our High Point neighbors knocked on our front door. This was in the spring of 2008, about a year after we had settled into our new High Point

The front yards of a for-sale housing block

home. We invited Rob and Heather Carballo in, and they proceeded to tell us how the High Point HOA board was making their life miserable. They learned that they had apparently violated an HOA rule and felt as if they were being treated like criminals as a result. The Carballos were living at High Point in part because of its diversity—exactly the kind of homeowners High Point needed—yet they were now seriously considering moving out.

As it turned out, the Carballos owned two homes at High Point; this was against the rules. They had been married only recently, and the house Heather owned at High Point had been too small for their newly combined family. So they had purchased a bigger house, near ours. They wanted to sell the first house, but by 2007, the home sales market was going in the wrong direction, so they decided to hold on to the smaller house and rent it for a while. This put them on the wrong side of the HOA rule that prohibited investment property in a High Point for-sale home.

My fingerprints were all over this. Not only had I written the rule, but the zealot pushing to enforce the rule who ran HOA worked for me. At NewHolly, one of our other mixed-income communities, investors had been purchasing some of the houses intended for homeowners. We had scrambled to change these HOA rules to prevent this behavior, and I made sure that the HOA rules[98] for High Point included a clause that kept investors from buying homes.

---

[98] SHA, as the developer, created and wrote the rules for the High Point HOA. These rules cover a myriad of subjects, from keeping cats on leashes (I'm not kidding) to putting away garbage containers.

So here were the Carballos, sitting in our living room, at the end of their rope. They had come to us as a last resort. I do not know whether they knew that Julie was a lawyer or that she had served as the general counsel for SHA for ten years. Either way, Julie has never taken well to bureaucrats running amok and enforcing rules in a foolish, harsh, and rigid way.

The Carballos were facing a stiff fine for choosing to stay at High Point. This community-minded couple, committed to living in a multiethnic neighborhood, was considering taking a big financial loss by selling both houses and moving out. But first they wanted to know if either of us could do anything about their predicament.

Over the next several months, Julie worked with a HOA subcommittee to review the rules. Despite being incredibly frustrated, she was able to get the rule modified in a way that allowed the Carballos some breathing room so that they could, on a temporary basis, live in one home and rent the other. They lived at High Point until 2019.

The Neighborhood Association

In thinking about organizations needed to manage High Point, we had to think about the diversity of people and personalities that would be part of the community. We knew that some people like to enforce rules, and some people see great value in getting to know their neighbors—and these people are not necessarily one and the same. In addition to creating HOA, we wrote up incorporation papers for a new organization we called the Neighborhood Association (NA).

We wanted to officially create an organization that would work to break down the class, income, and ethnic barriers we anticipated would be present in the new community. Our idea was that this entity would focus on building social networks through events such as community potlucks, clubs for mutually shared interests, block parties, and so on. NA leaders would be elected by those living at High Point, and the majority of the board would be made up of renters in order to keep homeowners from controlling the NA's operations. To provide this organization with a healthy annual budget, we taxed all existing High Point homes at the time of sale.

The voting system we created for the NA meant that leaders were selected either from a block or a set of blocks. This organization functioned for a number of years, but despite the attempt to stack its members in favor of renters, the homeowners always ended up in the driver's seat.

The NA operated until 2015, when it closed down. The reasons for the closure included changes in state law regarding the way funds were raised to support it (Washington's legislature prohibited charging sellers of homes in a community from paying a fee to the community when their home was sold) and the difficulty in obtaining reasonably priced liability insurance.

Nonetheless, the NA idea was kept alive by making the NA a standing committee of the OSA.[99] The committee members are no longer elected but participate if they are interested. The organization is now referred to as ECOSA, the Events Committee of the Open Space Association.

Seattle Housing Authority Management

Like many aspects of affordable housing, ownership and management of the High Point units is not straightforward. SHA does not directly control the rental units. To raise money for the construction of the site and the low-income units, SHA created two entities, High Point North Limited Partnership and High Point South Limited Partnership, and sold the bulk of ownership in these entities to for-profit companies. This is how capital is commonly raised for affordable housing.

The for-profit companies monitor the financial health of the affordable properties and hold veto power over major

---

[99] Carol Wellenberger, SHA, personal communication to author, May 2018.

Officer Kevin McDaniel is the longtime High Point community policing officer.

decisions in the operation of the housing. The arrangement allows the companies to obtain federal tax credits that lower their overall federal tax burden. In this way, SHA obtained additional capital that made High Point feasible. This deal lasts fifteen years, at which time full ownership of the units reverts back to SHA. During this fifteen-year period, SHA serves as a management agent and general partner, but it is the owner of the tax credits that has to approve major decisions.

Managing the Affordable Rental Housing

Managing 600 family rental apartments that are also home to 1,200 children under the age of eighteen is not a job for the fainthearted. For the last ten years Terry Hirata has ably carried out the duties of site manager for SHA. One aspect of Terry's job is conveying to families (the parents and their children) the community's standards for appropriate behavior for teenagers. Terry and his staff have made it clear that living at High Point is a privilege. That privilege can be forfeited if a family member repeatedly violates community rules or breaks the law. It is a harsh reality for a community the size of High Point that the management team needs to be the enforcer of community standards.

The SHA management team performs all of the other functions normally performed in managing rental housing, such as screening prospective tenants, maintaining the units, enforcing lease requirements, and collecting rent. SHA is expected to meet private sector standards for rental management, as its performance is monitored by the tax credit investors.

Seattle police officer Kevin McDaniel is the community policing officer at High Point. Kevin knows High Point well, as he has worked in the community for the last twenty years and lived at High Point for four years after the redevelopment. Over time, his role in the community has changed as the community itself has transformed. In the 1990s, one of his responsibilities was to serve as protection for the management staff when they made house visits to rental units. Now he accompanies Terry Hirata on house visits occasionally, getting involved only when there is criminal activity. "Normally only two or three families are a problem at one time," he said when I interviewed him in 2019. While Kevin lived at High Point, he realized how quiet the community was. "There is still some crime," he observed, "[but] actually less crime than the rest of Seattle." He feels that the community is working better as neighbors are taking responsibility. One way this is seen is that there is now enough trust between residents and civic structures that people call 911 and report problems with their neighbors. (Families who do not speak English have access to an interpreter on 911.) This is a big deal. People are taking "ownership of their community—something that has only come after many years. The management office and the police are headed in the right direction," Kevin said.

I asked him if he felt High Point was working. He addressed changes in perception and communications between low-income and middle-income families: "Each group is getting over their assumptions about the other group. Once they get beyond the assumptions, the community works much better."

Renter Households Today

Ethnic Diversity

By 2019, the composition of the community's low-income renter households had changed significantly from the beginning of the redevelopment in 2001. Somali is now the primary language for 29 percent of the population. Other East Africans make up an additional 10 percent. English speakers comprise 25 percent. The percentage of Southeast Asians has decreased over the last eighteen years to about 14 percent.[100]

---

[100] Seattle Housing Authority, June 2019.

TABLE 5. Language Groups of High Point Households (2019)

	Number	%
Amharic	13	2%
Arabic	9	2%
Cambodian	23	4%
English	149	25%
Lao	3	1%
Oromo	25	4%
Samoan	5	1%
Somali	171	29%
Spanish	15	3%
Tigrinya	15	3%
Vietnamese	54	9%
Other	16	3%
Blank	99	17%
Total	597	

The High Point Neighborhood Center

The High Point funding application to HUD called for a community center to be centrally located in the Commons Park. We had set aside $1.5 million in the budget for a building and we had designated a physical location, which we expected to donate, but that was about it. We did not know how much money would be needed to build it, where the money would come from, or other basics such as who would own and operate the building. About all we knew was that it was important to provide services to community residents and that some type of facility in the middle of the site was a good idea.

We chose to work with Neighborhood House, a local non-profit service provider that has traditionally operated services for Seattle Public Housing residents. Neighborhood House had recently built a building for service providers at Rainier Vista. And prior to redevelopment at High Point, Neighborhood House ran two Head Start classes in an old building on-site, which we had since demolished.

I began meeting weekly with Mark Okazaki, the Neighborhood House executive director; Ray Li, their development director; and Paul Fitzgerald from the development office. Our progress was slow, as we assumed—based on SHA's expertise at NewHolly—that SHA would develop the building and that some type of nonprofit board would manage it. But an external consultant advised us that Neighborhood House would be far more likely to mount a successful fundraising campaign, which led to the breakthrough decision to turn over the entire project to Neighborhood House.

Settling the question of ownership allowed a bold vision to emerge of a very green, multiuse facility, which would also serve as an environmental learning center. Mark and Ray went to work raising the funds to build a new center with public and private sources. The result was a bright, airy, $13.2 million, 30,000 square feet, Leadership in Energy and Environment

(LEED) Gold building with two solar arrays with a total of 384 panels on the roof (which generate 73 kw, or about half of the energy needed to operate the building) and a geothermal system for heating and cooling.[101]

Today, the building houses many of the essential services, programs, and activities that High Point neighbors take advantage of to enrich their lives. A partial list of these activities demonstrates both the community's diversity and the breadth of the building's use: Horn of Africa Playtime, Vietnamese Senior Group, La Leche League, Youth Empowerment and Leadership, Women's Night Out, Work Source Connection, English as a Second Language, Job Seekers Club, and much more.

Insights

Consider context. Those administering community rules need to understand the consequences of enforcing rules that were put in place for one purpose and do not make sense in another context. The HOA rule prohibiting investment properties in mixed-income communities has an appropriate place. However, when homeowners who are committed to the concept of the mixed-income community but are straddling real-life logistics are in effect penalized for wanting to stay in the community, common sense needs to prevail.

---

[101] Mark Okazaki, Neighborhood House executive director, email message to author, August 2, 2019.

Give renters a formal organization. From the earliest days of building HOPE VI communities, the housing authority has argued that it is not necessary to give a separate voice to the renters living in these communities, as the goal is to establish well-functioning mixed-income communities. The underlying thinking is that a council made up solely of renters would be counter to the whole idea of mixed-income communities. In the case of High Point, this decision should be changed. It turns out that there *are* issues that specifically affect renters. The 600 renter families at High Point should have their own council so they have a way to raise the concerns that affect them specifically.

CHAPTER 13

MY HIGH POINT NEIGHBORS

A block party with our neighbors on the street/alley where we lived.

In 2018 I interviewed several High Point residents to learn about what life at High Point was like for them. I either know the people interviewed from when I worked or lived at High Point, or they were recommended by friends who live at High Point. Janelle Gonyea, who heads the Management Trust, which manages the various High Point associations, provided some referrals for residents who moved to High Point more recently.

I spoke with people from varied backgrounds who had lived at High Point at different times in an attempt to provide a variety of voices, although space limits the number. I conducted all of the interviews, which have been edited for grammar and fit. The ideas and opinions expressed are solely those of the interviewees and do not necessarily reflect my own views.

Joyce Williams

Joyce has lived in High Point since she was a toddler. Her mother Sandy Taylor had moved the family into High Point in 1968. Sandy died a few years ago.

Did you feel safe at the old High Point?

Oh, man, old High Point was family. Everybody knew everybody. Everybody respected everybody, knew who their kids were.

How are you involved in the community now?

I sit on two boards. The first board is the Section 3 [prioritizes Seattle Housing Authority hiring from its low-income residents] board. I've been on that board for eleven years. I was just unanimously voted in on the board of directors at the Neighbor Care Clinics. That is helping me with my mom's legacy, as she was on the board that got the High Point Medical and Joe Whiting Dental Clinics established.

What's your relationship with your neighbors?

There is one family that's right across the alley from me; they actually used to live up by where Mom used to live when she was on Holly Street SW. So I've watched Eva [Joyce's daughter] and B. grow up together and go to school together. They're a Muslim family, and we get along great. When they first moved in right across the alley from us, A. was the baby, and I used to have fun seeing and playing with her. And I look at them now—gosh, she's in middle school! The people who moved in after them actually turned out to be their family friends that they knew in Africa. Every time they come out the door and I'm on the balcony, we always say hi to each other.

How would you characterize the relationship between home-owners and renters?

I get along fine with the owners that are right close by me. I honestly think it's like any community. It's just personalities, and either you rub people the right way or you don't. But as far as I can tell, we all get along fine. Eva and me go trick-or-treating to the homeowners giving out candy [laughs].

Are there changes that you'd like to see in High Point?

I wish we had more of a community feeling like we used to have. When I grew up, if I got in trouble down the street, I'd get it from everybody from where I got in trouble at till I got home, and then I'd have to deal with my mom on top of that.

The one thing I can say about High Point when I was growing up is: there was more respect for people than there is now; there was more trust than there is now. A lot of the difference, I believe, has to do with the way things have changed everywhere. You know, information is out there more and more, and things are talked about more than they used to be.

I love my deck [of her carriage unit above a garage], because I can sit out there when it's windy and rainy, and I don't get wet, and I can still smoke my cigarettes.

We put those decks on those units at the end of the alleys thinking that this was a way to have eyes on the alley and what's happening on the block.

Yeah, it is.

What do you like best about High Point?

The fact that I still have a roof over my head, because of how much I pay for rent, because my rent is still based on a subsidy. That is actually the one thing that Mom pounded in my head: you don't give up your place in High Point unless you know for a fact that you will be able to keep a roof over your head outside of High Point, and with the way my jobs have come and gone, that's what's kept me at High Point. You know, I'm poor [laughs], but at least I have a decent roof over my house. There are times that I wished that I could be rich, but then I think rich people have just as many problems as we poor folks do.

I have a story from when Eva, my daughter, was four years old. She'll be 30 in January. Where we lived in High Point, the front door faced a three-bedroom unit. One night after I finally got her down to sleep, it was about 1:30 in the morning, all of a sudden I hear *bap bap bap*—gunshots. I'm like, *Oh, my God!* I get on the phone to 911 and tell them someone is shooting up my neighbor's house. Eva comes running out of her room, and I throw her behind me on the couch. The cops came and dealt with everything, and for the next few days, we were all just kind of watching out for each other.

A few days later, it was summer, I had fallen asleep with my door wide open. I opened my eyes, and I saw my neighbor standing there with a shotgun in his hand. He looks at me and says, "You're okay. I've got your back." What else could I say but, "Okay. Thank you for having my back."

Let me tell you something, I've seen the good, the bad, and the ugly in High Point. As it turned out, [in that shooting] they targeted the wrong house, and the family that was living there at that time got moved out on an emergency move. I never saw him again, but I always remember "I've got your back," and his standing there with a shotgun in his hand.

Now I'm starting to see kids that I've watched grow up and have their own kids, and I'm telling them, "All right, I've seen you grow up, yep, so you know that baby's my grandbaby, right?" You know, teasing them, telling them their babies are my grandbabies. They're like, "Yes, ma'am, they are." [Laughs.] And they call me Nana Joyce.

Marilyn Myers

Marilyn purchased her new house in High Point in 2006.

I moved to High Point because I was interested in downsizing. I was just totally excited with the whole idea and with the plan and with the mix. I bought a house before it was built.

How are you involved in the community now?

I'm involved both formally and informally. Until the summer of 2018, I was a volunteer and then a teacher at the elementary school [West Seattle Elementary School in High Point], and that was one of the best parts of living here. I walk a dog, Gila, and the kids in the neighborhood would all say, "That's Mrs. Myers. That's her dog, Gila." If a kid crossed the street, I could say, "Look both ways," and because I was a teacher, they would. I loved volunteering at the school, and then when I became a part-time Title 1 Remediation Specialist, it made it even better. I was getting paid for work that I love to do anyway.

Along with that, I had met the Somali family that owned the little halal grocery on Graham [in High Point]. They were an extended family of siblings and aunts and uncles. From about 2008 to 2012, I probably tutored eight members of their family, including a former sister-in-law, because they were very anxious to improve their English literacy. Two or three of the boys were sent to Kenya for high school, and they came back ready to apply to college, and their skills were really high except for writing, and so I coached them in writing and they ended up being University of Washington (UW) students and graduates. The daughter worked at the store and then went on to finish the very difficult UW nursing program.

That's actually my next question. What's your relationship with your neighbors?

I love the fact that the neighbors here, people who choose to live here—especially now that it's not the recession, and they're not buying the houses just because they're cheap—are choosing to move to a community. They know that we can hear voices, that we have small yards, that we share a community, and so most of them are really ready to be neighborly. We share recipes and borrow sugar and do neighborly things. People invite us to events at their homes, and we invite them, and it's almost like the old kind of '50s-style neighborhood. When I hurt my knee this spring and finally came out walking again, they'd say, "We noticed that other people were walking your dog. Are you okay?"

Are you aware of the natural drainage system and how it works?

I feel like I've been the natural drainage system expert in residence.

Den mother?

Yes, right. When people move in, or when they're thinking about the neighborhood or even when they've come to look at houses on sale, and the real estate broker says, "I don't know anything about that," I would explain to them how the system worked and about the indigenous foliage in the swales. I love walking or running around the pond or watching kids bicycle around the pond. I've become familiar with several kinds of mushrooms that grow there in the spring and fall. I love watching the birds. There's a heron who comes for carry-out fish for dinner, and there are osprey and of course numerous fowl, various kinds of mallards, and seagulls.

Tell me about some of the people you know who rent at High Point.

I moved here for diversity, and I wanted to know my neighbors. At the corner of my street is a long-term renting Mexican-American family that I know very well, and their kids have been very helpful. They have five kids from 20 to 9, and I've been the teacher in a couple of their kids' classrooms, and they're very strong neighbors.

In 2010, I was walking my dog, and I met a young Somali woman (she was probably 19 at the time), crying at a bench. She had moved in with her auntie, and they had lived here quite happily until the uncle returned from Africa, and suddenly she didn't feel welcome anymore, because she was a very American child. She came here as a Dreamer when she was two, and the uncle wouldn't accept her as she was. She said, "I don't know where I belong. I wear jeans. I am a Muslim girl, but I'm not totally covered, and I go out with friends at night, and I don't have a place here." I loaned her a lot of long scarves to cover up when she went home. She moved to Kentucky or Tennessee to live with other families for a while, and then came back to live with other relatives. One day there was a knock on my door, and she moved in. From January until April, she lived with us off and on, and we call her our daughter. We helped her get a good job, which she's had for months, and she knows that when she needs anything, we're here to help her. I've learned so much from having a Somali daughter who's now 26.

How would you characterize the relationship between the homeowners and the renters?

I think you can't generalize. There are homeowners who have nothing to do with the renters who live in Polygon. Many of them don't know any renters. They don't interact, and they don't send their kids to the elementary school [in High Point]. Then there are homeowners who have sent their kids to the elementary school. Many of them are volunteers at the school. They've gotten to know the kids.

Do you feel safe in your home and in the neighborhood?

I feel very safe in my home and neighborhood. There was never a time that I didn't feel safe. I walk my dog at 11 at night. People are friendly and greet each other. Now I'm not vigilant enough, and packages frequently get stolen. The glass front door was broken—somebody threw something at it, but that was the first time in eleven years we've ever had any vandalism. We've never had any incidents with anything taken [from the house].

What do you like about High Point?

There isn't anywhere else, or I don't know anywhere else other than Columbia City, where I could have had these kinds of relationships. There's another Somali family of ten where I'm welcome at their house any time, and we share bicycles around here. I don't really want to leave, other than I need more rooms now.

High Point neighbors lining up for food at a community party.

Thu Thai Duong

Thu is in her late 20s and grew up in High Point. She now lives there with her son A. She is hired on a part-time basis to organize community events.

I'm a stay-at-home mom now, but sometimes I work on a part-time basis for the community as the event organizer. I like to do community things, and I was doing home health care for a while.

Even though back then [in the old High Point], there was a lot of crime going on, we knew who our neighbors were. We were like family. We lived right behind each other and we felt safe, because they're looking out for us, we're looking out for them. We knew when someone left town—who's going to Vietnam, who's going to Cambodia, how long they're going for. We looked out for them.

What's your relationship to your neighbors? It sounds like you don't have a relationship with them.

I don't have a relationship with my current neighbors right now. They're very closed-minded.

Do you know any of the homeowners in the neighborhood?

I do. I am a people person, so I like to be social with people. When I walk by someone's house or someone goes by my house with dogs or their kids, I'm like, *Hi!* I try to associate with them, and they know my face, they know my name. When I did the block parties, I met homeowners here, and so we had really nice get-togethers in the summer.

Are there any changes you'd like to see at High Point?

Yes, a lot. It's good that we're doing all these events for the community to get all of our neighbors out together. We have the Night Out block parties, kids' events, and family events, like movie nights at the park. It was nice, but it depends on the people if they want to participate. There aren't a lot of people who are willing to participate.

What do you like best about High Point?

I love staying in High Point. Everything that is built here is new. It's a whole new program, a whole new process of living here, new neighbors, new people, and they are always trying to create new projects to keep it alive here in High Point, so people don't get bored with it. We always have new projects and new events.

Your son is too young to go out to the park by himself now, but in a few years, would you feel comfortable letting him go to the park by himself?

I would not. I wouldn't feel safe, even when he's five. It's not the community, but it's the people. It's anywhere. It's a reflection of what's going on in the greater society these days. I'm scared for when he becomes a teenager. What's going to happen?

My childhood, I had the best time! You know, even though there were crimes going on, I didn't feel not safe. I felt like I knew everybody here, and they were here for each other. If I were to fall down in the street, my neighbor would call my mom and be like, *Your daughter fell.*

Now, even if my son is playing on my porch, I feel unsafe. I have to leave my door open. I have to leave all my blinds open. I have to open the window. I have to create a little gate so he doesn't run out in the outside of the porch. I just feel like someone could just snatch my son and run away, you know. I'm scared. It's not safe here. I don't take my son to parks here.

Helen Biersack

Helen B. moved into Phase II in 2011. She is an architect specializing in sustainability issues.

I first came to High Point as part of a tour back in 2005 or 2006. I was on the tour with a friend of mine, and I think they had Phase I open, and they took us by the pervious concrete street and Pea Patch and some of the rental units and then talked a bit about the rest of the plan for the community and the drainage system. Coming to live here was a little serendipitous. My boyfriend and I were renting, and we were being evicted.

In addition to the drainage features, what was it that appealed to you?

Just the fact that it was a green community and a mixed-income community. The fact that that was intentional was something that I liked and was drawn to, sort of the equity part of it, social equity. And then for T. [my husband's son], he was eight—all those parks to play in, a nice soccer field up the hill—we thought it would be great. There are tons of kids around. Unfortunately, as he grew older, he became less social, so he doesn't hang out in the neighborhood so much anymore, but I think it was really meaningful for him to be able to play with other kids in the community when we first moved in.

There were no fear or safety issues at all, concerns?

No, not for me.

Not for your husband?

No. You know, [my husband] had this rule when he was a kid: when the streetlights come on, you come back to the house. T. had trouble remembering that, so we'd have to go looking for him sometimes. But, yeah, when he didn't feel safe, he would come back home.

What other kinds of decisions did you see as a professional in your field that you responded to?

I personally responded to the whole project. The idea of low-income renters living with homeowners, the cultural diversity—I didn't know that that had existed in Seattle. I didn't realize that there was such a huge refugee population in Seattle. But I think it was a combination of that and the little pocket parks.

It literally was a big playground for T., and it was easy, close to the bus. I took the bus and still take the bus everywhere—hate driving—and so there are tons of convenient bus transit options anywhere I want to go. So the fact that it was a build green [area], they had the community solar project [on the roof of the Neighborhood Center], the Pea Patches—it was just a well-thought-out project. All the different pieces played a part, and the fact that it was affordable at the time. That worked out in our favor, and we'll be here for a long time.

How are you involved in the community now?

Right when we moved in, I wanted to join the Design Review Committee [of the HOA]. My background is in architecture and building, but that was a full committee, so I opted for the Finance Committee, which had an opening. I had my eyes opened to the world of HOA finance and the issues that you have to think about when you're living with a large diverse community, making decisions together. I joined that committee right away, so it had to be 2012, and I'm still on it. At some point during the process, [there was an opening in] the Design Review Committee, and H. asked if I would come on in the interim until they found somebody. I said sure, because I told her I didn't really have time to do it—but I haven't stopped doing that, and it's probably been three years.

Tell me about some of the issues faced by the Design Review Committee.

Paving, tearing up grass, completely swapping out plants. The design guidelines encourage native and drought-tolerant plants. We had one resident who took out all their lawn and bushes and planted rose bushes. That person got dinged for not complying, not having an application. Then we have to figure out retroactively: How do we make this work, how do we help the homeowners achieve their goals for their own private space within the guidelines of the greater neighborhood? Most of the time homeowners are pretty willing to do a few extra things to bring their yard into compliance, and other times it's a bit more challenging.

What's your relationship with your neighbors?

We've actually had a lot of new people move into our building—it's a fourplex. We are the original owners of our unit, and then J. next door to us is the original owner, and everybody else has rotated out. We participate in the Neighborhood Night Out, and that's part of how we've met some of our new neighbors this year, but they trickle in, and we've been trying to get together with quite a few of our neighbors. Scheduling stuff with people with kids is challenging.

Tell me about your relationship with low-income renters in the neighborhood.

I think there are assumptions that many homeowners make moving into the neighborhood, those who maybe are not original owners but didn't know what they were getting into, and

I think there's judgment. Some homeowners move into a community with an HOA thinking, "Oh, this is going to be great. Everything's going to be the same, and I don't have to worry about anything, because somebody else will take care of it for me," and that's not how it works.

Some families have a lot of kids, and their kids leave toys around. I think between renters too, though, there are issues. There are a lot of cultural differences that people don't understand, and that makes it challenging. Language is a barrier that makes it challenging. We make it a point to say hello to everyone. At the very least, most people know hello and a smile, and we're always out in our yard doing work and offering to help anybody else.

I think people want other people to be like them, and the rental communities are very culturally diverse and even the home-owners are not all alike, so there's a rift. I think it's a sign of sort of what's going on in the greater city, country, state, and world. There's a divide, and people are afraid of what and whom they don't know, and I think they make assumptions.

And living across the street or back to back with people of different cultures and ethnicity and income, does that affect their thinking at all?

I think over time it can. I think that's so specific to individual people. Some people are just curmudgeons and don't want to believe anything outside of what they originally believe and aren't willing to allow those barriers to break down, and other people are the exact opposite. So I think it truly is an independent thing, but also if you don't at least have the opportunity for different cultures, different economic groups to live side by side, you don't even have a chance; you can't break that down. You can't see that the other person isn't so bad, and they really are like us. They're just trying to make the best life that they can with what they have in front of them.

Everyone has heard of the *Seattle Freeze*: You come to the city, and the first two to five years, you don't know anyone, and there's this reluctance to take the next step in developing a friendship. I think that is independent of race, ethnicity, or age. It's just with Seattle being, especially now, as transient as it is and new people moving in, people feel isolated initially in a city where they don't know anyone. They have to slowly meet people and build connections, but people within the city also move around so much. I know for sure that on my block of sixteen or eighteen homes, [only] three of them have been there from the beginning. People don't stay where they are.

Where I grew up, I would get kicked out of the house to go play with anyone who was outside, and now we have this need to hover over our children and make sure that they're not getting into trouble, and it's completely different. I grew up in a neighborhood full of Italians, Greeks, Irish, Polish people. It was a very ethnically diverse neighborhood. We had neighbors who couldn't talk to each other because one spoke only Polish and the other spoke only Greek, but kids still played together. I think that's the power of young people in society where there are a lot of cultural and ethnic diversities, where language is an issue. I think that's where barriers can start to break down.

Did that happen with your son?

Yep.

When he was younger?

Yeah, absolutely.

It's not so much now that he's in junior high.

Yeah. When we first moved in, some of the younger kids started to get themselves into some trouble. You know, they'd steal each other's bikes, and there was some bullying happening and things like that. T. has chosen to stay away from it, so he doesn't hang out in the neighborhood anymore. He used to play basketball, and then a group of kids would come around and single him out, and he just didn't want to deal with it. He's come back to our house a couple of times upset and mad. He came back with puffed-up feathers, like he was going to take down the world, but he had no idea what any of it meant. He was just reacting emotionally, so we had to talk him off the ledge. I think one time he was threatened physically by a group of kids by the basketball court. Whether or not they were actually going to do anything, who knows, but T. came back to the house. J. had made him a wooden sword and shield when he was a kid, and T. came looking for the sword and the shield, and that's not how you solve anything. So we had a teaching moment with him.

We told him, any time you feel afraid, come tell us, and if we can talk to the kids, we'll talk to the kids, which is really embarrassing for him. I don't care. But, yeah, there's an opportunity with children to break down those barriers. If we have kids, we know what it's like to be a parent at the very least, and that's a connection, and when you don't speak the same language, it's hard to make those connections.

What changes would you like to see at High Point?

I'd love to see the socioeconomic and cultural barriers break down, but that's really challenging, because I don't know that people are going to stop coming and going. I'd like to see that both in the rental community and in the homeowner community. I think the more homeowners and the rental communities can interact and interface, the better it is for everyone in the neighborhood. But that will happen one at a time, I guess. Other than that, the neighborhood has issues just like every other neighborhood. I know they're always trying to improve it where they can.

What do you like best about High Point?

I like how walkable it is. I love the parks. I love the natural drainage system. I love the Pea Patches. I think they started doing a farmers' market with one of them, which is fantastic. I love the proximity to downtown. It's great. I feel like there's something for everyone. The big park in the middle, the Commons Park, you can do lots of different things in it, and then if you want a field, you can go up the hill to the fields. You can play basketball. There are sidewalks. I know that's not a big deal to some people, but I think it's great. There are a lot of neighborhoods without sidewalks.

Ethiopian woman in her 30s
Chose to remain anonymous

My family originally moved to High Point in 1992. We moved from the old High Point when the housing was getting torn down in 2006, and then several years later, we moved back into the new High Point. I lived at High Point all the way from three to eighteen. From there, I started going to Seattle University, but I was always back at home so I was still here.

Tell me about the nostalgia you say you feel for the old High Point.

I miss the community, and this is something that I hear from others as well. Regardless of the stigma [associated with old]

High Point, there was still a sense of safety and community, and it's not like that anymore. You know, I think it's the actual infrastructure of the buildings as well; everything's so close to each other, the mixed income. I remember seeing this outdoor billboard [marketing the new for-sale housing] in the new High Point that had this really thin white blonde woman dressed in business attire. So bringing in exactly that demographic … then our being treated like we should leave the neighborhood, and, it's like, *We were here first.*

Let's talk about the community. Did you feel safe when you were living here?

In the old neighborhood, I still felt safe. Again, I think that goes back to the sense of community, people knowing each other, knowing each family, as well as the Diversity Festival [an annual festival held in the old High Point].

What about after the redevelopment? Does it still feel safe to you?

It doesn't. And I say that because it was hard for me and I know for others, too, after the redevelopment. I've had to really comprehend and make sense of certain feelings and emotions that I have whenever I am in High Point, and there are certain new things that come with it. You have individuals now who don't look anything like you, who before wouldn't even drive into High Point.

They were afraid.

Yeah, right. They were terrified. Now here they are walking their dogs around, and then they're looking at us and telling us that we need to leave the neighborhood. You can feel the nonverbal communication. It's there. We had this one Fourth of July, in 2011, we were hanging out at the end of High Point on that hill that takes you down to Delridge, and a woman came by and goes, "You guys need to get out of my neighborhood and go back to your neighborhood." And we were like, *We grew up here.* The only reason why we had the transition—moving back into High Point—was because they tore down the neighborhood.

Last year, I was asked to speak at the Youth Tutoring fundraising breakfast, and I talked about the trees, because they are so powerful. The [saved heritage] trees are now the only way we know where old homes and old streets were. The trees serve as landmarks in the neighborhood.

There needs to be more of an effort of trying to bridge both communities and trying to create that unity again, so thinking about how we can still honor all people, how we can still honor community. Today it's one of those hit-or-miss things. If I'm walking down the street to a friend's house, it's really hit or miss if I see someone who's white that's walking by and they don't greet me or if I greet them. [Old] High Point was a very special place at the end of the day, even though it's torn down.

Helen Underwood

I moved into High Point in July 2007, at the very beginning, before we had finished streets, back yards, or a park.

And why did you move here?

I was freshly divorced, and I was rebuilding, and it was a really crappy time in my life. I first came to visit with a friend who lives in West Seattle. I was looking at townhouses in the area, and everything was ridiculously expensive. My friend said, "Hey, you know, there's this new development. It's a really cool concept. It's right in West Seattle. I think the houses are a little bit cheaper just because it's an experimental community." So I came out here with her and left with paperwork, and it was actually for one of the Polygon houses. Then the next day I came back just to do another sanity check and discovered this street. I threw away that paperwork and signed on for where I live now.

What was it about the community that attracted you?

I love the philosophy of it, and then obviously the draw of a new house, too. I don't know what I was expecting when I came in, but I was floored at how beautiful the neighborhood was, even with it not being finished. Lovely houses. You could tell there were going to be lots of little pocket parks. And then we walked around and saw the view of Seattle—just kind of over-whelming at first.

Are you involved in the community?

Not in an official capacity. I organize the block parties.[102] We do the Night Out every year. We've got a Facebook group going just for the people on the block, and I always do a big winter party that everyone comes to.

When I first got here, like I said, I was kind of starting over. When you get divorced, there's a separation of friends, and you end up losing a group of friends. So I came here, and I think partly because we were all moving in at the same time and also because this neighborhood attracts a certain type of person who's going to be more open-minded and, I think, tends to be a little more liberal and friendlier, everybody started clicking right away, and it became sort of an instant group of new friends.

People have moved in and out. I think there are only five houses on our block, if we count both sides, that still have the original owner. The other ones have turned over. As the original folks moved out, we got people moving in who were buying at a lower price, and they weren't as philosophically bought into the concept.

The former neighbors still come back and do all the neighbor-hood stuff with us, but it felt like it was slipping away a little

---

[102] In 2019, block parties were held on different nights throughout the community.

bit, and I didn't want to lose that, because this was my community and my new extended family. So I starting getting more involved with parties and making sure that we had communications going on. For a while, they had block captains, and I took that on for a while and kind of fostered the communication, and then that kind of grew into, *Let's have parties and socialize*, and I became very close friends with a few of the neighbors.

Do you know other renters?

Not that many. There are people we say hi to on the street. I'm horrible with names. I used to be pretty good friends with J., one of the renters who moved a few years ago. She was here when I moved in. But I've found I meet most people walking the dog, and some neighbors are not into the dog thing, and so we say hi across the street but they stay clear. If it's somebody who has a dog or who likes dogs, then you strike up the conversation and you tend to talk more. With the people renting, I've found that if they're dog-tolerant, we definitely talk more. Otherwise, they just kind of avoid me.

How would you characterize the relationship with the renters and owners?

Well, it's interesting, my experience versus what you see people complaining about on Nextdoor.[103] In the summertime, it can be

---

[103] Nextdoor is an internet-based community bulletin board that allows people to make anonymous comments about their neighborhood.

kind of rough around here—like, the kids are bored and they get into trouble. They're up late. Fourth of July is kind of an icky time.

But I've never had any issues with neighbors. We had a group of tweens this summer that were causing trouble, and eventually it got sorted out. But people get really pissed off and everybody grumbles, and then it goes quiet, and nobody really has any issues throughout the rest of the year. It's just in the summertime that you tend to hear the grumbling.

What do you like best about High Point?

The community definitely. There's a real sense of community, and it's not just the people that live on the block. People tend to smile and say hi to each other a lot more than I've seen in other neighborhoods. We're ten minutes from downtown; yet we have this wonderful sense of community that's usually in the 'burbs and sometimes not even there. I like the people that the community attracts. They're open-minded for the most part and tend to be more progressive. It's a little bit of a bubble.

Maybe you can help describe this, in terms of: people walk by, you're a High Point neighbor, there's kind of almost an obligation to say hello.

Yeah, I think so. I grew up partly in Texas, and everybody says hi to each other there. Even if they're going to stab you in the back when you turn around, they'll say hi and smile. I think after the [2016] election, it made me feel fiercely protective of especially the immigrants in the neighborhood. At that point, it's, like, I'm going to make even more of an effort to say hi, smile big, be genuine, and that kind of thing. It kind of felt like people were rallying around the neighbors after that all went down. Signs were going up in the windows, like *Safe House, You are welcome here*, and that kind of stuff.

Are they still up?

Yeah, there are a few that are still up. There are some on our block.

Describe those signs a little bit for me.

There are some that say, *This is a safe house. You are welcome here.* After some attacks had happened—not in this neighborhood, but just around the country—there is one sign, I can't remember exactly what it says, but it's in three or four different languages. That was interesting during that time because there are homeowners and renters, and people were being extremely supportive of each other.

Richard Landes

Richard purchased a new townhome in 2014 located in Phase II.

Was buying a good investment?

I would say so. It's gone up about fifty percent since I bought it.

Are you involved in the community?

I'm the treasurer on the HOA. I wanted to get involved right away, and I wanted to understand better how the finances were managed in the community. I began to realize how complicated High Point really is, because of the structure. There isn't one budget. There are twenty-six budgets, and they're really complicated, and it's kind of messy, so it needs oversight to make sure it's taken care of. I've been doing that for two and a half years now, and it's been a learning process.

Tell me about the relationship you have with your other immediate neighbors.

I was pretty close to a couple who are my neighbors. We would hang out together, because we live in townhouses that are right next to each other. We would see each other working on our lawns and [them] maybe playing with their children, and it was great. Then across the way, I know one of the families who had been on the HOA board, and I know another family who were also on the board, but they moved away. A lot of people are selling out and buying new homes. I know some other people in single-family homes across the way. Honestly, I've gotten to know a lot more people than I ever have in other neighborhoods that I've lived in, because of the close proximity and the logistics of the neighborhood. It's real easy to come up to people and say, "Hey, how's it going?" I would say I probably know 15 to 20 people. I wouldn't say I know them well enough to have dinner with them, but I definitely know who they are, engage in conversations with them, and feel comfortable about that.

Do you know any of the renter families?

I don't, and, you know, I don't really know how to get to know them. Like I don't know what to do. I'm this old white guy. I feel sort of awkward. How do you do that? I'm not making excuses. I'm just saying that's how it is.

I think there are tensions between the communities, because of the perception that people living in Seattle Housing Authority buildings don't manage their children the way they "should." So people see children running around doing things that a lot of homeowners don't understand why. I have some concerns. You see small children running through the streets and stuff like that, and so that's one big issue.

Are you aware of how the natural drainage system works here?

Yeah, absolutely! Love it! The realtor did a good job and talked to me about the natural drainage system, and it finally started to sink in for me like, *Oh, wow, this is a significant thing!* I love that about the community, and I just cringe when I see people washing their cars and stuff like that. All the oil spills on the pavement from junky old cars drives me crazy, but it is what it is. I'm an extreme environmentalist. That's my thing. I put solar on my home as soon as I moved in.

What do you like best about High Point?

The number-one feature for me is the trees. I mean, there's no comparison. I've been in so many nauseating suburban neighborhoods where they cut all the trees down. You go into High Point, and it feels like you have this strange experience of, *Oh, this seems like a really old community, but all the buildings are brand-new.*

I ride my bike down the street. I see these beautiful old-growth trees. I see immaculate lawns. I see underground power, which you don't see in the city. It's like heaven on earth to me. Whereas most developments, they cut down all the trees, they put aboveground power, and it's just horrible.

I don't experience fears or concerns walking around at all. There have been some incidents of gun violence from time to time but, you know, it happens throughout the city, so it doesn't feel like it's overwhelmingly a problem for me at all. So, no, I never feel at risk or concerned or fearful.

CHAPTER 14

CONCLUSION

I am reluctant to pass judgment on High Point as a grand social experiment; however, I can't help but share a few observations to close this book. The comments of the High Point neighbors I interviewed span the range of opinions of how the community is working. Families continue buying new homes and moving into new market-rate apartment buildings. These families are giving the community high marks with their financial commitment as they buy or rent. High Point is no longer a community to be avoided.[104] That is a big change in nineteen years and reflects great progress—the community is headed in the right direction.

Looking back, four things we got right from the early planning years stand out to me.

1) We mounted a well-conceived, extensive, and at the same time authentic outreach campaign. As one leader of a nearby neighborhood told me, his neighbors were initially

---

[104] A decrease in crime statistics is one way to measure progress, although immigrant families at High Point may be reluctant to call the police. The Seattle Police Department crime report shows some activity at High Point, but it is comparable to the low activity reported for all of West Seattle. Seattle Police Crime Dashboard, accessed August 23, 2019, https://www.seattle.gov/police/information-and-data/crime-dashboard.

fearful of redevelopment, but that fear dissipated as they heard more and more about the redevelopment plans. When I first started the job, I gave multiple presentations to every organization I could find in West Seattle. And our stakeholders group, the Partnership for High Point's Future, gave the West Seattle community leaders a front-row seat and a say about the plans for the new community.

2) Another idea well worth replicating was our decision to expand the members of our weekly architectural and engineering meetings to include experts who normally would not have been invited to these meetings. Because of this, we carried out integrated design with consultants who saw the possibility for expanding beyond a traditional redevelopment.

3) Our partnerships with the city's public utility department resulted in important breakthroughs and spawned the natural drainage system, a concept that showed how storm-water drainage can be used to enrich the streetscape and add home sale value while solving an urban infrastructure problem. Building this system took many years and required both sides to operate out of their normal comfort zone, but in the end the system created has turned into a national model of storm-water management.

4) Our three-themed approach to problem solving—engaged community, healthy environment, and quality design—resulted in a number of important innovations, including

the building of sixty Breathe-Easy Homes. These specially outfitted houses eased the burden of asthma in the lives of children and their parents. The community also deserves high marks for building Energy Star homes across the site.

A major concern I had from the start regarded our ability to create value for homebuyers. Thanks to our effective strategies and the strong Seattle housing market, we developed a community that is sought out by homeowners and that weathered the great housing recession.

The outside world has certainly noticed High Point. High Point has been given twenty major awards. Two organizations put the redevelopment through an especially rigorous process before deciding it was worthy of their award. Both the Rudy Bruner Award for Urban Excellence (a Silver Medalist), and the coveted Global Award for Excellence from the Urban Land Institute, sent teams of experts to carefully study the site and interview neighbors and local leaders.

Though no longer a resident, I frequently walk around High Point. I do this in part to check out new for-sale homes that, as of the fall of 2019, are still under construction, but I do this mostly out of the pride I take in how the community turned out. I love to see the tree canopy, especially the birch trees that follow the site's water line to the pond. I find it reassuring on rainy days to see rainwater flowing through the splash blocks and the openings in the curbs that move the runoff water from the street flow into the swales. I am pleased to take in the level of maintenance of the parks and planting strips. I'm sure there are some yards that are not well maintained, but overall the place looks good.

I worry that the site is too big and that there are too many restless teenagers. I used to think, "All it takes is for a few kids to act out to turn around the community's reputation." Now I'm pretty sure the community is self-reliant enough to handle its problems. I'm still fearful that too many incidents could turn into a problem. Not unlike the fear parents carry for the well-being of their children, it never goes away.

I believe we've succeeded in our goal of fitting the redeveloped High Point into the fabric of West Seattle. High Point no longer carries a negative stigma. It is now, with an enhanced green element, just another West Seattle neighborhood.

Acknowledgments

Special Thanks

Stephen Antupit
Zach Chupa
Kathy Gwilym
Ellen Kissman
Jim Krieger, MD
Doug Larson
Stephanie Lawyer
Marilyn Meyer
George Nemeth
Peg Staeheli
Julie Wade

Ron Atkielski
Vincent Bachman
Helen Biersack
Dana Bourland
Rita Brogan
Willard Brown
Carol Brown
Tom Byers
Stephanie Caldwell
Jean Campbell

DeVonne Chambliss
Brian Cloward
Richard Conlin
Andrew Cronholm
Casey, Kathleen and
Dillon Crowell
Jared Cummer
Rome Doraty
Al Doyle
Thu Thai Duong
Andrea Dupras
Roger Fujita
John Funderburk
Thomas Gerard
Sibyl Glasby
Jonell Gonyea
Barbara Gray
Kathy Gwilyn
Joanna Hankamer
Rich Hill
Terry Hirata
Matthew Hoffman
Heather Hutchison

April Jackson
Tom Johanson
Bethany Kelly
Bill Kreager
Robert Landes
Al Levine
Ann-Marie Lindboe
Andrew Lofton
Harry Matsumoto
Miranda Maupin
Kevin McDaniel
Sean McKenna
Mai Nguyen
Greg Nickels
Mark Okazaki
Shukri Olow
Doug Orth
Nancy Owens
Guy Anthony
Parramore
Luisa Perticucci
Doug Repman
Cynthia Schick

Denise Sharify	John Taliaferro	Marcia Wagoner
Zev Siegl	Cassandra Tate	Carol Wellenberger
Bianca Siegl	Sandy Trent	Richard Wolf
Dan Smerken	Lanh Truong	Chuck Wolfe
Wendall Smith	Helen Underwood	Bob Wyda
Tim Spelman	Stephanie Van Dyke	Ann Fiske-Zuniga
Matt Suhadolnik	Catherine Verrenti	

Special thanks to the Seattle Housing Authority for permission to use several photographs that appear within this book.

U.S. Senator Patty Murray was helpful in maintaining federal funding for housing. She is shown here in front of some rental housing. We gave hundreds of High Point tours.

APPENDIX

Replacement Housing as of 2015

Reprinted by permission of the Seattle Housing Authority

Frequently Asked Questions

Why doesn't Seattle Housing Authority replace all of the housing it is tearing down in the same location?

The HOPE VI program does not support replacing all of the original low-income housing on site. One program goal is reducing the concentration of low-income housing. Seattle Housing Authority also supports the transformation of these communities from low-income enclaves to mixed-income neighborhoods.

In addition, Seattle Housing Authority does not have access to funding that would make this possible. Capital grants received annually from the US Department of Housing and Urban Development (HUD) are not sufficient.

Why isn't all of the housing being replaced as traditional public housing?

Traditional public housing requires ongoing annual operating subsidy from HUD, which has been steadily eroding over the past ten years as the federal government has been allocating less and less funding to traditional public housing. The federal government is not supporting the construction of any new public housing.

What is the role of Housing Choice Vouchers (Section 8) in replacement housing?

Housing Choice Vouchers are used to provide ongoing operating subsidy to replacement housing units owned and managed by Seattle Housing Authority or other nonprofit organizations. Rather than assigning the voucher to a specific tenant, the housing authority assigns the voucher to an apartment. In this way the housing provider receives enough subsidy to make the unit available to extremely low-income residents, those with incomes under 30 percent of the area median income.

Are people who use Housing Choice Vouchers able to find suitable housing in Seattle?

For the most part, residents who choose to accept a Housing Choice Voucher rather than relocating back to a redeveloped community have been able to find the kind of housing they want. In some cases, they have chosen to relocate outside of Seattle, to be near jobs or family.

Why doesn't Seattle Housing Authority simply renovate and remodel the existing communities such as Rainier Vista, instead of tearing them down and building new housing?

There are currently no federal housing programs that would provide sufficient funding for renovation of these worn-out housing units. Also, revitalizing these communities provides the opportunity to create somewhat denser, more urban neighborhoods with new social services to support low-income residents as they work toward increased self-sufficiency.

Why is Seattle Housing Authority replacing traditional family housing open to anyone on the agency's waiting list with housing that is restricted to the elderly?

Elderly single-person households have always been a large component of Seattle Housing Authority's resident mix. They also make up a large portion of the waiting list. By building housing specifically for the elderly, the agency is taking advantage of federal funding for this type of housing while preparing for the future when additional housing for the elderly will be needed even more than it is now.

How is the HOPE VI program in Seattle different from HOPE VI in other parts of the country?

The HOPE VI program does not require that housing authorities replace all of the housing that is lost to HOPE VI redevelopment. Consequently, in many parts of the country, HOPE VI really does result in a reduction of the amount of housing available to those with very low incomes. In Seattle, however, the housing authority has made **a commitment to one-for-one replacement**, and is carrying through on that promise.

Commitments

In some cases, revitalization efforts mean a decrease in the number of public housing units in the communities traditionally owned and managed by Seattle Housing Authority. However, even though there will be fewer units of housing for extremely low-income residents in specific communities, the overall number of units throughout the city will be maintained.

Seattle Housing Authority has an absolute commitment to one-for-one replacement of all housing lost through revitalization. Replacement housing will continue to be affordable to

Seattle's most impoverished residents—those with incomes at
30 percent or below the area median income.

Criteria

Replacement housing must meet four criteria:

- It must consist of specific, identifiable housing units.
  Replacement housing does **not** include Housing Choice
  Vouchers that households may use to rent in the private
  housing market.
- It must be affordable to extremely low-income residents—those earning less than 30 percent of the area
  median income.
- It must be guaranteed to be available to extremely low-income tenants well into the future. This is generally at least
  40 years.
- The household's portion of rent and utility payments
  must be no more than 30 percent of their income.

Replacement housing is not always the same as traditionally-
defined public housing. For example, some replacement
housing is owned and managed by nonprofit organizations
with subsidies provided by the housing authority. Capital or
operating subsidy that allows rents to be kept affordable for
extremely low-income households may come from the federal
public housing program or it may come from other federal
housing programs.

Financing

Housing providers serving extremely low-income house-holds, including Seattle Housing Authority, need financial help because the rents these households can afford will not cover the cost of constructing or acquiring, and managing and maintaining the replacement housing.

Seattle Housing Authority uses a variety of methods to finance and sustain replacement housing. This includes traditional public housing, funded by the federal government, which provides ongoing capital and operating subsidy.

In addition, construction funding may be provided by grants under the U.S. Department of Housing and Urban Development's Hope VI Program. Acquisition funding may come from bonds.

In other cases, Seattle Housing Authority:

- Contributes funds to assist with construction costs of some partnership projects, so that development partners do not have to borrow as much money. With less to be repaid, lower rents can be charged.
- Assigns Housing Choice Vouchers to some units within partnership buildings to make the units affordable to extremely low-income residents.

- Provides Housing Authority land to partners at below-market or no cost, enabling them to finance projects or obtain grant funds that would not otherwise come to Seattle.
- Purchases housing with bonds and assigns Housing Choice Vouchers to those units, or obtains HUD approval to convert the newly-purchased units to public housing.

Replacement Housing

The Seattle Housing Authority Board of Commissioners approved a replacement housing plan for the High Point redevelopment, to serve residents whose incomes are below 30 percent of the area median income.

In total, 716 units will be replaced. This includes 425 units on-site at High Point. 350 of these are operated by Seattle Housing Authority, and serve extremely low-income households. In addition, Providence Health Systems has built and leased Elizabeth House, a 75-unit apartment house for low-income elderly residents.

The remaining units may be replaced on-site or off-site, in buildings owned by Seattle Housing Authority, or in partnership with another housing provider.

Replacement housing results

As of the end of 2015, all 716 units of housing affordable to extremely low income households have been replaced.

Name	Manager	Units	Types
High Point	Impact Property Management	350	24 1-bedroom 115 2-bedroom 184 3-bedroom 24 4-bedroom 3 5-bedroom
South Shore Court	Seattle Housing Authority	8	5 1-bedroom 2 2-bedroom 1 3-bedroom
Elizabeth House	Providence Health & Services	75	74 1-bedroom 1 2-bedroom
Gossett Place	Low Income Housing Institute	12	12 Studio or 1-bedroom
Haddon Hall	Plymouth Housing	10	1 Studio 9 1-bedroom
Rose Street Apartments	Bellwether	4	4 2-bedroom
Lam Bow Apartments	Seattle Housing Authority	50	9 1-bedroom 29 2-bedroom 12 3-bedroom
Kenyon House	Bellwether, Building Changes, Sound Mental Health	18	18 studios
Delridge Triplexes	Seattle Housing Authority	6	6 2-bedroom
McDermott Place	Low Income Housing Institute	10	10 studios

Park Place	Retirement Housing Foundation	26	26 studios and 1-bedroom
Pardee Townhouses	Bellwether	3	1 3-bedroom 1 4-bedroom 1 3- or 4-bedroom
Casa Pacifica	Bellwether	11	11 2-bedroom
Bellevue and Olive	Bellwether	5	1 2-bedroom 4 3-bedroom
Villa Park	Seattle Housing Authority	5	3 2-bedroom 2 3-bedroom
Longfellow Creek Apartments	Seattle Housing Authority	9	4 1-bedroom 5 2-bedroom
Mercer Court Apartments	Bellwether	3	3 2-bedroom
Cascade Court	Bellwether	5	3 2-bedroom 2 3-bedroom
Dekko Place	Compass Housing Alliance	5	5 2-bedroom
Bergan Place	Compass Housing Alliance	8	8 2-bedroom
Nhon's House	First Place	5	5 3-bedroom
Lakeview Apartments	Low Income Housing Institute	5	5 2-bedroom
Crestwood Place	Mt. Baker Housing Association	6	6 2-bedroom
Brettler Family Place II	Solid Ground	21	12 2-bedroom 9 3-bedroom
Emerald City Commons	Mercy Housing NW	12	6 2-bedroom 6 3-bedroom
Imani Village	First Place	8	8 3-bedroom
The Parker	Bellwether Housing	8	8 2-bedroom

Leshi House	Seattle Housing Authority	28	28 1-bedroom
Total		716	

ABOUT THE AUTHOR

Tom Phillips, a Seattle native, has enjoyed a decades-long career as a planner and manager, serving in local government as well as being a consultant to private developers specializing in citizen involvement, new urbanism, and affordable housing. The pinnacle of his career was leading an almost decade-long project for what would become the largest housing redevelopment in Seattle's history, High Point. Tom's background includes earning an MA in Urban Affairs and Policy Analysis from the New School for Social Research in New York and a BA in Economics from Williams College in Massachusetts, as well as stints with both the Peace Corps in Liberia and as a Vista volunteer, where he worked with low-income families as a community organizer. He has spoken at conferences around the country on smart growth and green development. He lives with his wife Julie in the Capitol Hill neighborhood of Seattle. They lived at High Point for four years.

INDEX

Page numbers containing "n" indicate a footnote.
For example, 96n59 refers to page 96, footnote 59.

Made in the USA
Middletown, DE
26 April 2020

91963522R00166